Writing Like a Taller Person
The Best of Frank Cerabino

To Charlie & Gail —

Happy reading,

By FRANK CERABINO

The Palm Beach Post

Design by MARK BUZEK

Copyright © 2011 by *The Palm Beach Post*

All rights reserved. No part of this book may be reproduced in any form or by any means without the prior written permission of the publisher, except brief quotations used in connection with reviews, written specifically for inclusion in a magazine or newspaper.

Printed in the United States of America

1st printing 2011

Library of Congress Control Number: 2011939273

ISBN: 978-0-615-54321-5

Originally published in *The Palm Beach Post* from 1991 – 2011.

$9.95 U.S.

Chapters

	Introduction	1
1	**Taking notes at the carnival:** A columnist's haven	6
2	**Century Village:** Can we all just get along?	21
3	**Berm abrasion:** Cautionary tales of communal living	30
4	**New Yorkers:** Refugees from a hallowed land	38
5	**Car troubles:** Real people in a wheel jam	47
6	**Palm Beach:** "An island off the coast of the United States"	63
7	**News from the strip club:** Somebody's got to do it	82
8	**Natural disasters:** The hurricanes of 2004 and 2005	90
9	**Man-made disasters:** Trump and Limbaugh	96
10	**Man-made disasters, Part II:** The Election of 2000	108
11	**Marriage (and divorce) Palm-Beach-County style**	117
12	**Political sideshows:** Public servants of note	128
13	**Divine interventions:** What in the name of God is going on here?	135
14	**Boca Raton:** Artificial enhancements in progress	141
15	**Good deeds in our midst:** People you'd be lucky to meet	149
16	**Frankly personal:** Taking the job home with me	159
17	**Notes from hell:** Sparring with readers	168

INTRODUCTION

When I started writing a local news column for *The Palm Beach Post* 20 years ago, a reader warned me not to get too comfortable.

Writing a newspaper column is like being married to a nymphomaniac: It's only fun for the first two weeks, I was warned.

OK, well that didn't turn out to be true. It's still fun – even though the performance anxiety hasn't abated in all these years.

I wish, instead, that somebody had warned me from the start that, sooner or later, I would have to address my height.

For the record, I am 5-foot-9, which I have always considered to be on the shorter side of average, but certainly within a standard deviation of normal. Let's put it this way, nobody has ever approached me to ride thoroughbred horses, rescue a child from a well, or serve as the Secretary of Labor in the Clinton Administration.

I had no idea that writing a newspaper column would involve addressing my height. Had I known, I would have been more prepared.

I got my first inkling of trouble in 1995, when a Palm Beach Community College student named Mary Flesch decided to deliver a eulogy of me as her final exam in a speech class. Flesch, an enterprising young woman, got the material for her speech by calling some of the people I had written about in recent columns.

One of the people she called was John Sansbury, a former Palm Beach County administrator whom I had freshly irritated in a column. Sansbury was more than happy to offer up a dry-eyed tribute for my pretend-eulogy.

"He had that Napoleon syndrome," Sansbury said, "because he's such a short person, shallow person and he seemed to want to take it out on anyone larger than him, which in life, was most everybody."

Flesch got an "A." I got the news. Height matters, at least when it comes to writing barbed commentary, my favorite kind.

Years later, I showed up to speak at a luncheon meeting for a local organization. The woman who invited me had only seen my mug shot in the newspaper, and when I introduced myself to her in person that day, she blurted out her surprise.

"You write like a taller person," she said.

I'm not sure if it was meant as a compliment, but over time, I've regarded it as the most gracious assessment of my columns during these two decades.

Culling a sampling of them for this book hasn't been easy. Writing three to five columns a week for this long in a place as interesting as South Florida creates an overflowing pool of abhorrent behavior to consider.

So if your favorite column is not among the 74 in this collection, I understand. You don't have to tell me. I already know. I've come up short again.

CHAPTER 1

Taking notes at the carnival
A columnist's haven

Stampede at Wolfie's: What Boca won't do for a free bite
July 1, 1998

What price pastrami? Eat free or die trying

Free food — to die for.

"Get me some water," the old woman says, in a voice croaking with need and wooziness, as she sits, half-dazed on the sidewalk outside Wolfie Cohen's Rascal House in Boca Raton. I've been standing in the noonday sun for about an hour, slowly roasting along with several hundred other people, nearly all of them retirees. We form a snaking line around the restaurant, which opened for business Tuesday with a sure-fire way to draw the multitudes.

Free food. All day from 11:30 a.m. to 9:30 p.m.

"When you say 'free,' the people come out like bugs," says Helen Riordan, the woman standing in front of me.

Free food, yes. But with a price.

How long would you be willing to stand in the cloudless, shadeless summer swelter for a free lunch? One hour? Two hours? 'Til you're like that old woman sitting on the sidewalk, teetering on the precipice between consciousness and corned beef?

I showed up at 11:30, with the foolish notion that somehow I'd beat the rush. But by the time I arrive, the restaurant's parking lot is full, and two Boca Raton police officers are stationed at the restaurant's front door to prevent a stampede from those left outside to wait in the sun.

Inside, the restaurant has reached its 350-seat capacity with people

Taking notes at the carnival: A columnist's haven

Customers line up at the door of Wolfie Cohen's Rascal House. Hundreds were lined up outside for opening day. (Bob Shanley/The Palm Beach Post)

who started waiting in line at about 8 a.m. We can see them through the glass windows, munching on the garlic pickles, fresh-baked rolls and pickled tomatoes. Their mouths are filled with overstuffed pastrami sandwiches, potato pancakes and strawberry cheesecake.

And we are slowly wilting, huddling under umbrellas, cowering from the sun, and trying to stay optimistic despite the sweat that is rolling down backs and puddling under armpits.

"At least you know they won't be waiting for their checks. That shaves off five minutes," says Bernie Levine, of Boca Raton, who is standing near me with his wife, Estelle.

"It's not the free food we're here for," Estelle says. "It's the fun."

Another man overhearing her pipes up: "What else have we got to do?"

One of the few people who apparently does have something else to do is the woman behind me, Debbie Lata of suburban Boca Raton. She has to take her 12-year-old son, Joey, to the orthodontist at 1:50 p.m. in Coral Springs. But she's got time for the free lunch, she figures. Right?

"We were going to stop for McDonald's," Lata says.

And as the time ticks away, she starts wishing she did. It's getting close to 1 p.m., and we're still not inside yet. She keeps checking her watch and talking about leaving. But she's suffered too much to quit.

A police officer brings a cup of water out to the old woman sitting on the sidewalk, and suddenly there's a chorus of "water, water" from the line. Within minutes, Rascal House workers are walking down the line with pitchers of water and cups.

By now, I've become friends with all the people around me. We're sharing something akin to a warlike experience. We can tell things to each other we probably didn't think was possible an hour ago.

"You know," Bernie Levine tells me, "I haven't used deodorant since World War II."

I'm telling Riordan and her friend, Gale Dawn, about my children, my wife's work and the merits of putting raisins in stuffed cabbage.

As we get close to the front door, we're met by a stream of departing diners, who are leaving with toothpicks on their lips and doggie bags on their hips.

"Worth waiting for," a woman announces to us.

"Do they have flanken?" Bernie asks.

"No flanken," she says, "but you can get a half a chicken."

A half a chicken. We're buoyed by the good news. Word has filtered out that the restaurant has provided a slimmed-down menu for its free-food grand opening. Thirty items, we hear.

"As long as we can have the desserts," Gale Dawn says. "Just give me the desserts."

The original Wolfie Cohen's Rascal House, on 172nd Street and Collins Avenue, is a deli restaurant institution in Miami Beach. While other restaurants, including one in Deerfield Beach and Delray Beach, use the Wolfie's name, they are not affiliated with the Rascal House.

The Boca Raton restaurant is run by the same organization as the original Rascal House, although its menu has been augmented beyond its Jewish deli roots to include a Chinese salad and some Italian entrees, including pizza.

We're almost to the front door when a short, gray-haired woman with a yellow sweater steps up next to us.

"Will I ever get in?" she asks.

"In about two hours," Bernie says, pointing her to the back of the line.

The little woman smiles.

"I thought you were my cousin," she says, acting like she was about to step under the rope and cut in line next to us.

But Helen Riordan shakes her head and tells her to go to the back of the line.

"I don't want to end up with a bullet in my head," Riordan says.

Meanwhile, in front of us, a man is yelling loudly to the police officers.

Something about how he wasn't cutting in line and how he was waiting with a wheelchair all the while. A few minutes later, we're out of the sun, beyond the police checkpoint and into the lobby for the final 10-minute wait. And much to everyone's surprise the little woman with the yellow sweater has managed to sneak in with us past the police checkpoint.

Bernie gives her a stern lecture about line cutting. But she ignores him, staring straight ahead as if she doesn't hear him.

Debbie Lata, upset that she probably missed her son's orthodontist appointment because of waiting in line, tries to shame the line cutter into leaving.

But the woman won't budge. So Lata goes off to tell a police officer to remove her from the line. But the officer, already overwhelmed with his assignment for the day, has no stomach for manhandling the pint-sized grandma back into the sun.

After an hour and 33 minutes, I'm at the counter, munching on pickles, buttering rolls and feeling my sweat-soaked undershirt dry with a caked-on coolness.

"My wife would kill me if she knew I was here," says my counter-mate, Sam Epstein of Kings Point in suburban Delray Beach, as he bites into his brisket.

Sam dropped his wife off for a series of medical tests at the hospital. Then he darted to the Rascal House. She thinks he's still at the hospital waiting nervously for her.

"How about some more cole slaw here?" Sam says to our waitress, as he motions to the nearly empty relish tray we've both been ravaging. "It's mostly water."

Ah, life is good here on the inside. I look out of the window, where I can see the line of people shuffling on the sidewalk.

"It took me an hour," Sam explains. "I held my ground."

Matzo ball soup, a Reuben sandwich and blueberry cheesecake: A lunch I'll surely pay for, one way or another.

Lata, who is sitting at a nearby table, calls up her son's orthodontist, trying to reschedule his appointment. No way.

Oh well. At least she's enjoying her Reuben.

Across the restaurant, the Levines are eating with Gale Dawn and Helen Riordan. Estelle's got the half-chicken. Bernie's got a sandwich. And Gale and Helen are sharing their meals.

I say goodbye, and Gale stops me.

"Will I see you later?"

"Later?" I ask.

"For dinner," she says. "I'm coming back here with my daughter for dinner."

The Notorious Rodney: Most famous cross-dresser in town
Sept. 18, 1992

Transvestite burglar is back — and looking for something to wear

Women's clothing stores beware.

Rodney Lowery's back.

The notorious transvestite burglar, queenpin of a shadow society of men who steal women's clothing to wear in beauty pageants, is on the street again. He's fresh from a two-year prison stretch and showing signs that he's got nothing to wear.

Palm Beach Gardens police officer Robert Wummer arrested Lowery this week after a pre-dawn shopping spree at a Loehmann's Plaza clothing store.

"I know it's the real Rodney," Wummer said. "I saved his picture."

There are many pretenders to the throne.

Rodney Lowery is to transvestite burglars what Jesse James was to train robbers.

For years, other transvestite burglars have used Rodney's name after being arrested. It has given Lowery the supernatural ability to be both behind bars and still on the street breaking into clothing stores.

The real Rodney sometimes goes by the name Christian Dior. He lists his religion as "Holiness" and his occupation as "baby sitter."

(Transvestite burglar baby sitter. Now is that a TV sitcom idea or what? "He's so good with the children, Jill. I know that, Jack, but I'm tired of needing new underwear every week.")

A couple of years ago, fingerprint experts had to be consulted to separate all the real-Rodney cases from the wannabe-Rodney cases.

Still, it wasn't an exact science. Prosecutors estimated the real Rodney had at least six felonies and about a dozen misdemeanors under his garter belt.

Prosecutor Ellen Roberts figured it was time to send him for a long stretch in the crossbar hotel.

Although police say that local transvestite burglars have stolen millions of dollars in clothes — most of it handed off to fences — the case that brought Rodney down was a cheap one.

Just a couple of stolen rhinestone tiaras.

Rodney said the tiaras weren't stolen; they belonged to the winners of the Miss Divinity and Miss Gay Black Essence beauty pageants.

The jury crowned him a felon. Rodney compounded his problems by showing up in court dressed in a chartreuse crepe-de-Chine pantsuit, one that had been reported stolen in a smash-and-grab two nights before trial.

It looked like Rodney was going to be pressing license plates for a long time. The prosecutor was talking about using a habitual offender provision in the law, something that could turn a two-year sentence into 10 years.

"We're going to try to remove Rodney for a while," Roberts had said. "He's never been to prison before. It might have a greater impact on him than 30 days in the local clink."

Apparently not. The judge gave Rodney 4 1/2 years, rather than 10, and because of the marvels of prison crowding, Rodney was sentenced on July 24, 1990, and a free man again on Sept. 1 of this year. The two years he spent in prison kept him arrest-free for exactly two weeks.

That's when police say he and two of his buddies took a 5 a.m. shopping trip to Loehmann's Plaza.

Yellow Cab driver Nolan Teter was just sitting there waiting for a fare when he heard glass break and an alarm sound from Colby's Women's Apparel.

Teter radioed the police after seeing three men run from the store.

"It made my day," Teter said. "I wasn't making any money that morning. I was just sitting there."

Palm Beach Gardens officers chased the stolen car into Riviera Beach, where their cars collided. Lowery was in the front passenger seat. The $6,605 worth of stolen clothes were in the trunk and back seat.

"It was sportswear and dress wear," manager Adele Goldberg said. "Most were something a woman would wear to a fine restaurant or a theater."

Wummer, who arrested Lowery before, was surprised to see him out of prison so soon.

The cabbie had known about Lowery but didn't realize he was one of the men arrested until later.

"That's great," Teter said. "I've been thinking that these guys would probably not end up doing much time. But if that's Rodney Lowery, he'll have to do a lot of time for this, right?"

We'll see.

Lowery posted $1,000 bond on the grand theft case and was released from jail later that day.

Free, pending trial. He's out there. Somewhere.

And if you're in the women's clothing business, you've got to be hoping that Rodney already has a few nice outfits to wear in court.

The Pig Lady of Loxahatchee risks it all to capture Bobo, the escaped tiger
July 16, 2004

Baby the pig was Bobo bait, but lady bitten

Somebody needs to speak up for The Pig Lady.

I call Linda Meredith the Pig Lady because it seems like a fitting moniker for someone who drives a Cadillac with a live pig in the trunk. I suppose I could call the 40-year-old Loxahatchee woman Pork-in-Boots, but the English word for trunk might be a little too obscure.

The important thing at this point is clarity and for people to get a deeper appreciation for the civic can-do attitude displayed by the plucky, resourceful Meredith.

She has become the other bizarre pet owner in the sad saga of Bobo, the escaped tiger of Loxahatchee.

And, I believe, The Pig Lady has been greatly maligned.

"I hear the activists are upset," Meredith said. "Well, I'm an activist, too."

While others were wringing their hands this week over the unsettling possibilities posed by a 600-pound tiger on the loose in their community, Meredith sprang into unilateral action.

She came up with a plan to use her photogenic 5-month-old pig named Baby as a squealing dumpling of tiger bait.

"I used my animal instincts," she said. "You need live bait. I was going to eat the pig anyway on Halloween. It's a party roaster pig."

(Somewhere, PETA people are vomiting on their soy flakes.)

In the kind of activism you just don't see every day, Meredith proposed tethering her pig to a tree, then twisting the piglet's ears and yanking its hind legs as a way to transform her animal into a kind of biological dinner bell for the roaming tiger.

Unlike the tiger's owner, Steve Sipek, who actually shares his bed with his menagerie of jungle cats, Meredith's world view of her animals is somewhat more protein-based.

"Everybody eats," she explained.

(By the way, Baby's middle name is "Back" and last name "Ribs.")

When The Pig Lady drove her Cadillac to the search perimeter and produced her 30-pound trunk passenger for martyrdom, she not only was turned away but also became the target of an animal cruelty investigation by the Palm Beach County Animal Care and Control Division.

Is this any way to treat a good Hamaritan?

"Carrying an animal in a trunk in 90-degree heat, where it's probably 140 degrees inside, is not acceptable," said Diane Sauve, the division's director.

The Pig Lady explained that the trunk of her Cadillac is airconditioned.

(I must have missed a Loxahatchee episode of the MTV show *Pimp My Ride*.)

OK, so maybe the airconditioning extends only to the back seat. But in The Pig Lady's defense, it was less than a five-minute ride from her home to the search area, and she has been willing to demonstrate the conditions herself.

"I offered to get in my trunk," she said, "but nobody was willing to drive the car."

Nevertheless, Meredith said she won't contest the pending animal cruelty charge.

"It wasn't my intent to make the pig suffer," she said. "I was in the wrong, and I violated the law in the process. But I'm guilty without intent."

Bobo was shot and killed the following afternoon when the tiger allegedly made an aggressive move toward game officers searching for it.

"I hope they learned their lesson," The Pig Lady said. "I was the National Guard here. They needed live bait, and I was willing to pay the price."

Taking notes at the carnival: A columnist's haven   15

How much should salon pay for a bad hair day?
May 6, 1992

Jury: Bad frost job not to dye for

The Palm Beach County Courthouse was teeming the other day with tales of murder, broken business deals and rotten marriages.

But somebody else will have to tell you about them, because I got wrapped up in the trial about the woman with the hair problem.

Missy Freshour is her name, and what a great name it is for a wannabe blonde who got what the beauty industry calls "overprocessed" during a $65 frost job at the JCPenney hair salon in the Palm Beach Mall. The hairdresser who did it — here comes another great name — was a woman named Toni. (Is there a surplus of beauty professionals whose first names end with the letter "i"?)

Toni left Missy's chemically soaked head under the dryer too long, and Missy ended up getting mega-frosted. Her hair started falling out in clumps, which led to an emergency clipping of her shoulder-length mane to something in the Peter Pan range.

Missy sued the store and turned down a $2,000 settlement offer for a chance to plead the agony of bad hair before a jury.

How much do you compensate a person who is forced to go around with a bad haircut?

I have no idea. I rarely think about my hair. I don't condition it, never blow-dry it, sometimes forget to comb it and have remained immune to hair fashion for a couple decades.

I realize this may be aberrant behavior.

That's because my wife is a hair person who labors under the heat of hair dryers and the constant disappointment of not getting that elusive style she finds on magazine models, whose pictures she clips and saves.

When one of the women in my wife's family gets a haircut, it requires team counseling before and after. It's like they have to talk each other off the ledge every time. ("No, I think it looks good. I think it looks really good. I mean it.")

So I went to Courtroom 311 looking for what the courts had to say about hair — figuring it would lead to something between the minimal figure I would put on a bad haircut to the six-figure verdict someone in my wife's family might dish out.

Boy, there was a lot of non-litigable bad hair in that courtroom.

The lawyers looked like Sy Sperling's Hair Club for Men models. In the "before" pictures.

Missy's attorney, Thomas Kingcade, is a rapidly balding man.

"My wife's been trying to get me to get those hair plugs," he told me during a break.

Fortunately, he resisted. (Those transplants end up making a scalp look like a rice paddy.)

On the other side of the room was defense attorney Robert Ponzan, who has one of those plastered helmet-topped hairdos usually found on television anchormen and Ken dolls. Atop his head is a gleaming silver dollar-size circle of scalp, resembling the spot in a forest where the plane went down.

Freshour, 33, who has had a year to grow out of her frosting debacle, looked tonsorially blessed compared with these two guys.

The six jurors looked fashion impaired. No blondes with big hair. And the foreperson was a woman with a no-nonsense, close-cropped Afro. Two bad signs for Missy.

She needed jurors who looked like Circuit Judge Lucy Chernow Brown. Brown's got some hair.

Big brown hair. It's teased, shiny and 3-D.

The judge seemed attentive as Kingcade waxed poetic to the jury about hair and the meaning of life.

"If you look good, you feel good," the attorney said. "If you feel good, that's what life's about."

(Is that from the Bible? St. Paul to the Brillcreams?)

He told them his hair-as-identity theory, citing entertainers Crystal Gayle, Diana Ross and Cher. He told them about O. Henry's *The Gift of the Magi*, a hairy love story.

Then he went too far: "It's a disfigurement to her, just as the loss of an arm would be," he said.

Give Missy $15,000, Kingcade told the jury.

Ponzan, the JCPenney lawyer, conceded that the frosting "did not reach a good result" but said the damage should be worth about $500 to $1,000.

He cited the lyrics from a Randy Travis country-and-western song:

"Honey I don't care/ I ain't in love with your hair/ And if it all fell

Taking notes at the carnival: A columnist's haven   17

out/ I'd love you anyway."

Pretty lame. Those C&W guys all wear hats.

The jury spent about 20 minutes deliberating, before deciding on $2,500 — a figure closer to the defense's liking.

The short-haired foreperson, Elaine James, put it this way:

"It's just hair. She didn't lose a limb; it was just hair."

Irritating newspaper columnist sends Canadian packing
Oct. 17, 1999

'Something must have happened to you with a Canadian'

"After 14 years of wintering in Florida, Dartmouth Snowbird Lea Forbes says she and her husband are selling their Juno Beach house and saying good riddance to the Sunshine State for good - all because of one irritating newspaper columnist."

— Item in a Canadian magazine

I was mystified when a reporter from the Canadian political and satirical magazine *Frank* notified me about the story he was writing.

"Are you sure it's my columns?" I asked him. "There are plenty of other reasons why somebody might not want to live here anymore."

"No," the reporter, Cat Sullivan, said. "It's specifically your columns that are driving her out."

I explained to Sullivan that it's unusual that anyone would feel so singled out.

"I'm the local chapter president of a mythical organization called the Citizens Against Virtually Everything," I explained. "So I only have time to poke fun at Canadians maybe once or twice a year."

The last time was in August, when I reacted to a tourism story that claimed Florida was losing Canadian visitors because other sunny spots were offering better bargains.

So I proposed an All-Expenses-Eliminated Palm Beach County vacation for Canadians, a cheapskate's delight.

This was "the last straw" for Forbes, according to the magazine story.

"Furious Lea, who isn't overreacting at all, thinks the ungrateful Yankees should show a little more deference to their northerly invaders – after all, she's been dropping upwards of five figures into Florida coffers every year," the magazine story continued.

(My guess is two of those "figures" she's counting are to the right of the decimal point.)

Naturally, I had to talk to this woman, who was still at her summer house near Halifax, Nova Scotia. At first I reached her phone answering machine.

"You can call collect," I told her machine, trying to say it without any trace of mischief in my voice.

"I can't take it anymore," Lea said, calling back on her own dime.

"Why do you keep reading the column if you don't like it?" I asked.

"I keep reading it because I say, 'This man can't be this bad.' I keep looking that somehow you will find something in your heart to say something good about Canadians," she said.

"Why would I want to say something good about Canadians?" I said. "I don't say something good about anybody."

Forbes said she's putting her Juno Beach home on the market when she comes to Florida for the winter.

"We're going someplace else — outside Florida," she said.

"You don't have to leave Florida," I said. "My column doesn't make it out across the whole state. You'll be safely out of range on the west coast of Florida."

"No, we're leaving the state," Lea said.

Lea said she'd leave sooner, but she and her husband have a golf club membership at Ballen Isles this winter.

"What could I do to make it up to you, Lea?" I asked.

"You can't," she said. "You can't smooth it over. Something must have happened to you with a Canadian. You've had a bad relationship with a Canadian."

Clearly, I wasn't getting through to Lea.

"Lea, have you ever laughed at anything I've written?" I asked.

"Never," she said.

Lea suggested I use my column to write an open apology to Canadians.

"But if I do, how will you know?" I asked. "You said you're never reading it again."

"I have American friends who will read it to me," she said. "They'll let me know."

So if any of those friends are out there now, please pass this on to Lea: I hear Arizona's warm in the winter.

John Glenn's return to space: A plot to jettison elderly?
Oct. 25, 1998

What good can come from old people in orbit?

As an aspiring senior citizen, I'm voicing my concern about NASA's plan to launch John Glenn into space again.

For months now, we've heard straight-faced scientists talk about the need to explore the effects of space travel on senior citizens. I find this very disturbing. Why would senior citizens want to travel in space? Many don't even like to venture on I-95 anymore.

When I get old, I want to go out for lunch — not for launch.

And it would seem like the $500 billion cost of this trip could better suit seniors by spending it on more practical, and relevant, research — such as designing a Viagra pill that doesn't have the hour waiting period.

I suspect a hidden agenda.

Putting senior citizens in space orbit sounds to me like the 21st-century equivalent of shipping off old relatives to a South Florida condo.

Perhaps next century, South Florida's demographics will be getting younger and younger. And then ungrateful children, still eager to put some distance between them and their aging parents, will have to think of something more humane than packing them on rafts and sending them out to sea.

I can almost hear my future: "Listen Dad, you and Mom would be happier on the space ship. No yard to mow. The space walks will be easier on your knees, too. And with those space suits, you'll never have to worry about incontinence."

I can see my wife and me running afoul of cosmo board regulations and grousing about the rising cost of Tang. I can see myself shouting into my helmet microphone, "I'm weightless, and I can't get down!"

And it all will have started with the launch of the 77-year-old Glenn.

He should have just said "No."

The whole thing's a sham, anyway.

Glenn supposedly had very important experiments to perform in space. But then without announcement, NASA canceled one of the two primary tests Glenn was supposed to perform.

Scientists were going to check the effects a natural hormone would have on his sleep patterns.

But after all this hoopla, it turns out that Glenn isn't fit for the test.

Why? Probably because he's too old.

Which just goes to prove my point — space is no place for senior citizens.

You want to study why old men go to sleep in the middle of the day?

Forget about space. Go to the Boynton Beach Mall.

The place is packed with old guys sleeping on wooden benches while their wives shop.

Old men don't need hormones to keep them awake. They just need their wives to stop dragging them to the mall.

I can't envision anything good coming from sending senior citizens in space. And I keep worrying about what humorist Al Franken wrote in a prescient essay published before NASA announced Glenn's trip.

In what now sounds eerie, Franken pointed out that two huge drains on the federal budget are NASA and Medicare and finding a way to trim costs of both programs would be a boon to taxpayers.

Franken suggested using ailing senior citizens as space explorers. Launch them, send them where no men have ever gone — and don't worry about bringing them back.

A disposable space program would bring cost savings for NASA and Medicare.

Franken was joking. But what once sounds funny sometimes become reality.

In a couple of decades, I'll be part of the biggest generation of senior citizens this country has ever seen. Something will have to be done with all of us when we become drains on the economy.

You see what I'm saying?

We may have to take up space, just because we take up space.

So don't expect me to be applauding John Glenn on launch day. I wish him well.

But mostly, I wish he weren't going.

CHAPTER 2
Century Village
Can we all just get along?

Century Villagers turn century vigorously, head home by 12:05
Jan. 2, 2000

The ball drops —
but not the seniors at this soirée

I wanted to bring in the New Year at some place I would always remember.

So I went to Century Village. It seemed fitting, seeing as how we're straddling the century. And I figured that spending the evening with the revelers at the county's most well-known retirement community would serve as a bridge to both the past and the future.

"Try my noodle pudding," Dorothy Schreiber told me, soon after I arrived at the party room at the West Palm Beach community's main clubhouse.

Dorothy was at Table 38, where some seat jockeying was still going on.

Century Village New Year's parties are meticulously organized.

First of all, there's a lottery drawing in early December. There are only 1,000 seats in the two clubhouse party rooms, and 15,000 residents in the complex.

So, the first hurdle is getting picked in the lottery — or figuring out a way to circumvent the lottery. Then a couple weeks later, the lottery winners enter a second drawing that gives them the order in which they choose their table's location.

For the price of a ticket, partygoers get a live three-piece band, party hats and noisemakers, ice and bus transportation to and from their nearby condo buildings.

"I called my daughter in Maine and told her I was going to a big affair at the clubhouse," said Vince Sicliano. "'Guess how much it costs?' I asked her.

"She said, 'Two hundred dollars?'"

Tickets are $5.

As soon as the doors opened at 9 p.m., the partygoers started filing in, toting whatever food and drink they intended to consume during the next few hours.

Everything from hot casseroles to Publix deli trays to homemade cookies made their way to the tables, along with bottles of champagne and lots of ginger ale.

The dance floor was never empty, beginning to fill as soon as Al Matos and his trio struck up the first song.

"You have to play what they want," Matos explained during a break. "They want lots of fox trots, mambos and cha-chas."

The band seemed to reach its first peak with *Besame Mucho*, which caused the dance floor to overflow, making couples find dancing room in the narrow aisles between the tables.

Everywhere I went, someone old enough to be my mother was insisting I have something to eat.

As Esther Kanterman tried to get me to eat some of her liver spread, she told me what many others did — that their second life, the one they found in Florida at Century Village, had been a nice surprise.

"I felt like I started my life over here," said Kanterman, who met her second husband at the condo. "People on the outside have no idea what it's like here. When they call it Century Village, it's because you can live to be 100 years old here."

There was no dimming of the lights on this night, and no long breaks or soft ballads for the band. This was a vigorous assault on midnight, a three-hour marathon of noshing and dancing.

Keep moving, keep moving.

There was talk about the new gym that will be built here this year, and how handball courts will replace some of the shuffleboard courts.

"When I was 18, I threw a party for my mother when she was 50," said Mary Anne Dimperio. "I did it because I thought 50 was old and she didn't have much more to live."

Now, 80 doesn't sound too old to Dimperio.

As midnight approached, the dance floor became congested again. The band did the countdown. Pods of balloons dropped from the ceiling.

By 12:05, the people were sucked out of the room and toward their condos, as if with a powerful vacuum.

But before their welcomed release, the crowd whipped itself up for a final rousing display of energy as the band segued from *Auld Lang Syne* into *The Battle Hymn of the Republic*, which amazingly was danced to in a snaking, singing conga line.

Glory, glory hallelujah.

Growing up in Century Village? It's against the rules — and human decency!
Nov. 1, 1995

Century Village baby may find life a bowl of prune pits

Today, a Century Village condominium board will have to do its duty.

Kick the baby out. Undoubtedly, there will be talk about the importance of rules and the pitfalls of precedent during the Andover E Condominium Association board meeting in suburban West Palm Beach.

Ignore one infant in Century Village, they'll say, and the next thing you know, we'll be up to our restrictive covenants in diapers.

And, let's face it, the last thing Century Village needs is more incontinence.

But the real reason why the 6-week-old daughter of Chuck Herman, 69, and his newlywed wife, Lyda, 22, shouldn't stay is much more basic than that.

Chuck thinks it's just jealousy that's fueling today's board discussion. That other retirees are envious that Chuck married a woman who is — in Chuck's words — "a young girl."

While it's true that his new wife, Lyda, barely passed the child ban at Century Village herself, I don't think that's the issue.

And I don't doubt that many of Chuck's neighbors were surprised to find that he wasted no time in demonstrating that he had consummated his December marriage to the woman who is 47 years his junior.

But the real reason why little Mary Danielle Herman must be cast outside the gates of Century Village has nothing to do with envy.

It's simply a matter of being humane.

No baby has ever grown up in Century Village.

Many people have gone through their second childhood there.

But none has had to endure her first.

Who knows what kind of anthropological mutations might germinate from a childhood spent in Century Village.

No telling what might happen if little Mary has a Century Village imprint on her Wonder Years.

It would be a dangerous experiment, perhaps a South Florida version of that cautionary tale of the child raised by wolves.

Now, don't get me wrong. I'm not comparing Century Village residents to wolves. For one thing, wolves don't cough a lot in the morning.

All I'm saying is that nobody knows what kind of child might be molded in that kingdom of speed bumps, guard gates and multiple grandmas.

Who can say how well adjusted a child would be after being subjected to years of contentious condo board meetings, Depression-era reminiscences and never-ending medical complaints?

The child is bound to grow up feeling odd, chronologically ostracized and too embarrassed to admit, "I've fallen and I can get up."

That would be bad enough.

Century Village: Can we all just get along?

But then little Mary will be doubly traumatized when she becomes school age and ventures into the outside world, a world that will certainly seem strange to her.

A world where people pedal bikes that have two, not three wheels.

A world where kids play a strange game called tag, but know nothing of the game she knows best: shuffleboard.

A world where there's no such thing as a low-cost "early-bird" school lunch at 9:30 a.m.

She'll be unfamiliar with the ebb and flow of daily life outside the gates.

And her new world will assault her with the grim truths in life: That there's no such thing as a free trolley. That she really doesn't have superhuman hearing, after all. And as for big bands, sorry, they're not coming back.

She'll have too much to learn and unlearn.

It's a long way from the prune pit to the mosh pit. From prescription drugs to nonprescription drugs.

"No, Mary," they'll say. "It's a lemonade stand, not a Medicaid stand!"

What a shock it will be to find out that "cola" is a drink, not a Social Security cost-of-living allowance payment.

Or to realize that it's Luke Perry, not Perry Como, who is the hunk.

Chuck Herman plans to fight any move to boot him and his young family from Century Village.

He says he can't afford to leave the one-bedroom, one-bathroom apartment he's had for the past 24 years.

But in another sense, he can't afford to stay there, not unless he's willing to take his chances that somehow little Mary will grow up to be a normal little girl.

Inside Century Village?

It sounds like a long shot.

Run, Chuck. Run. That's my advice.

Gather up your family, catch the next trolley and don't look back.

Ashes kick up stir at Andover H building
Feb 14, 2001

'This is supposed to be Century Village, not Cemetery Village'

To everyone else, they look like growing trees, but to Brenda Banas they're dead neighbors. Banas gazes out her kitchen window overlooking the grassy courtyard area outside the Andover H building at Century Village in West Palm Beach, and has a troubling vision:

The orchid tree is Sid's sister. The magnolia, Sid's mother.

Sidney Mann, a beloved resident of Andover H, had shared a condo with his mother and sister, and when they died, he had their ashes strewn outside the condominium at the foot of newly planted trees.

Before Mann died last month, he requested that his cremated remains be given a similar memorial outside his condo.

And at a meeting of the 26 unit owners, a voice vote honored Mann's request.

At least that was the plan.

But that's when Banas began her campaign to end turning the grassy courtyard area outside her window into what she calls "a memorial park."

"This is supposed to be Century Village, not Cemetery Village," Banas said. "If it was my husband, I wouldn't want to have him out there."

Banas' fight has angered and surprised some of her neighbors.

"Sid was a terrific fellow, and he deserved to be buried there," said George Katzoff, the building's co-president. "He did all the landscaping and watering here.

"I look out at the tree and see beauty. I don't see the person."

Katzoff wondered if Banas was motivated by her dislike for Mann, who was a former treasurer on the condo board while Banas was the secretary.

"She and him didn't get along so well," Katzoff said.

But Banas said the opposite is true.

Century Village: Can we all just get along?

"A lot of times, I used to open my kitchen window in the morning, and say, 'Hi, Sid,'" Banas said. "Now, I open my window and he's not there. It's sad. But knowing his ashes are there would disturb me even more."

Banas wanted the memorial to be planted out of her sight, on a strip of grass bordering a canal and a chain-link fence, rather than in the landscaped communal courtyard that Mann maintained for his neighbors.

"They promised me that they would try to put him out by the fence. But others said, no, he had to be in the back with his mother and sister," Banas said.

The showdown got more heated as Banas complained up the ladder of Century Village's hierarchy and eventually to the county health department.

"I don't know why she has a bug . . . about Sid's ashes," former building president George Coahn said. "It's not a burial. We're just going to strew his ashes and nobody would know about it. Nobody would even know the ashes are there."

Banas, whose daughter died at 36, said she still can't stand going back to the site where her daughter's ashes were strewn. So she wasn't about to make believe a third memorial site out her window wasn't going to bother her.

"Their attitude was that it's just another tree," Banas said. "But I guess I'm one of those loudmouths not afraid to buck the system. I spent too many years being a people person."

This week people gathered outside the condo for a small memorial service for Sid Mann. His ashes were scattered around a newly planted bush.

But Banas didn't see it. Mann's memorial planting isn't in the same grassy courtyard with his mom's and sister's trees.

Mann's spot is out by the fence, across the parking lot. Banas said she's satisfied.

"I can't see it from my apartment," Banas said. "So I don't worry about it."

Orthodox resident uses condo as makeshift synagogue
March 3, 2011

'This is the greatest threat to the Village we've ever seen'

A Jewish civil war brewing in Century Village took a road trip this week to a Palm Beach County code enforcement hearing room, turning what is normally a sleepy venue of mostly empty seats into a mob scene of agitated retirees who tested both the limits of the building's fire code and each other's patience.

For weeks, residents of the condominium complex near West Palm Beach had been spreading the word to show up for the hearing on whether resident Issac Feder was improperly using one of the two condos he owns at Century Village.

Feder, 64, part of a small but growing sect of Orthodox Jews in Century Village, is a snowbird from Monroe, N.Y., who lives part of the year in a unit in the Kingswood building. But he owns another unit in the adjacent Golf's Edge building, which he and the other members of his religious sect have turned into a makeshift synagogue for the past two seasons.

Men dressed in traditional black garb and formal hats walk from other buildings in Century Village to conduct twice-daily prayer services in Feder's spare condo.

This has infuriated other condo residents, who are mostly Jewish but not Orthodox and don't want their building turned into an ultra-religious house of worship. And they've complained to the county, which initiated a code enforcement action against Feder.

"It's really not about zoning," said Sam Koenig, 64, an Orthodox Jew who lives in a different Century Village building and is sympathetic with Feder. "This crowd doesn't want this because it reminds them of an Eastern European shtetl, and makes them feel as if they're going back in time."

It wasn't hard to find confirmation of that opinion.

"I see their women davening and dressing like they're in Alaska," said Frances Merel, a Jewish resident in a nearby building. "I don't want to see it. They feel like the rules aren't for them. They're arrogant."

Her husband, Maynard, chimed in: "If they win, I'm going to turn my apartment into a mosque."

Jewish residents at Century Village talk freely about their condo community being overrun by the more zealous members of their own religion, whom they view as clannish and disrespectful of social norms — most notably, turning community pools into ritual cleansing baths.

"If they can get three or four people on the board, they can get control of a building," said resident Elaine Brown. "And then they can change the rules. This is the greatest threat to the Village we've ever seen."

Aron Sandel, one of the seasonal Orthodox Jews who lives in Century Village, says most of his critical Jewish neighbors are overreacting to people who are simply practicing their religion.

"We don't have weapons. No guns. Everything is quiet," Sandel said. "In order to pray, we need a minyan, and that's 10 men. Sometimes we have a hard time making the minyan."

The group has shunned the Orthodox synagogue outside the gates of Century Village. Last year, when the dispute began, Feder said he was too frail to walk outside Century Village to pray, so he used his spare condo as a gathering spot.

But he now says he sometimes lives in the spare condo, a claim that may be significant in the legal argument of his lawyer, Esther Zaretsky, but is scoffed at by his neighbors who showed up in droves on Wednesday.

"There was a big propaganda about this," Feder's wife, Judith said. "They want to show we are wrong."

Golf's Edge president Cookey Courier, a Jewish snowbird from Michigan, helped spread the word about the code-enforcement hearing with fliers advising residents to meet at the clubhouse and use carpools to get to the hearing.

The crowd overwhelmed the zoning room's capacity of 320 people. Villagers lined the walls, spread several deep on the wings and spilled into the hallways of the county's Jog Road building.

The fireworks, though, never really developed, because Feder's lawyer was able to postpone the matter, which brought groans from the audience.

"This is what they do," Courier said. "They postpone, postpone."

Carolyn Ansay, the special magistrate hearing the case, said she was sympathetic to all those who had packed the hearing room expecting a resolution.

"There's never been a code enforcement case that garnered the attention of this one," she said.

Maybe next time the county could find a bigger room, she told the crowd.

Marian Watnick, who was standing near the front, shouted a suggestion to the magistrate:

"What about the convention center?"

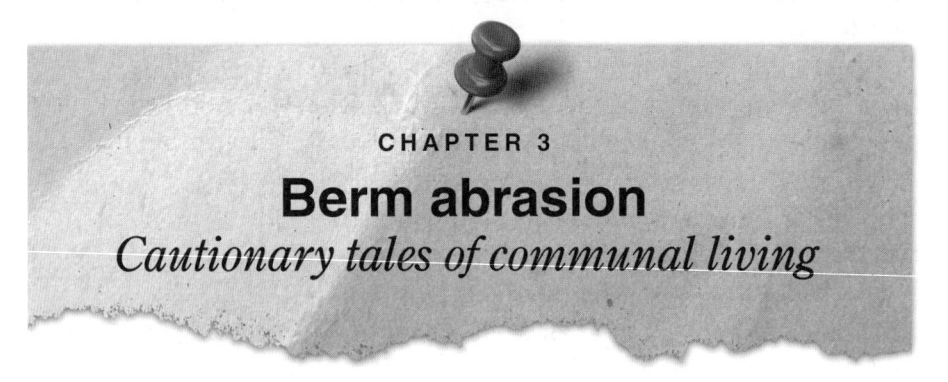

CHAPTER 3

Berm abrasion
Cautionary tales of communal living

At Kings Point, the show must go on, just once
Sept. 6, 1995

'We do musicals, because that's what keeps people awake'

The phone lines have been buzzing at Kings Point. Negotiations have been touch and go.

Will the Kings Point Players be denied a second night to stage their original World War II musical revue, *Was Kilroy Here?* And will the condo theater group be allowed to hire an outsider to play the piano for the production?

No outside piano players, says Artie King, president of the condo board in Kings Point, a sprawling complex of 13,000 retirees in suburban Delray Beach.

"We're overrun with piano players here," King said. "They should be able to find a resident to play the piano."

But Frieda Rothberg, who's playing Bette Davis in the Kilroy show, says the theater group has already gone that route.

"We used to have piano players from Kings Point," she said. "But the last two died. So we hired somebody from the outside."

Somebody young. A guy in his 70s.

The battle over the theater group made front-page news this month in the condo's newspaper, *The Kings Point News*. The newspaper published an open letter asking the community to let the show go on for a second night.

"One night would jeopardize this production as we cannot cover our costs," the letter written by Rothberg says.

The theater group has staged two performances a year for the past 14 years. The group charges $2 per ticket, and the shows play to near-capacity audiences in the condo's 1,300-seat theater.

The group pays for its own production costs, gives 25 percent of the gate to the condo for use of the hall and donates the rest to charities.

"We're not looking to make money, just to perform," Rothberg said. "It's something to make us happy, instead of sitting around and watching television and growing old, we're growing younger."

The group rehearses all year for the show, writing their own sketches and rehearsing songs.

"We do musicals," Rothberg said, "because that's what keeps people awake."

Anybody in the condo can join.

"Some people are 90," Rothberg said. "We have people with Alzheimer's. We don't throw them out. We put them in the chorus."

Sounds so benign. But in the condo world even benign organizations can be wrapped up in layers of political intrigue.

"Last year, we had one of our shows on a bingo night," Rothberg said. "You never do that, but we did, and we drew 700 people."

Bad form. And this season, the Players requested one of their shows to be on a Monday — a movie night at the condo.

King, the condo board of governors' president, says movies shown in the big theater are too popular to preempt for the Players.

"Everybody looks forward to the movie," he said.

And besides, he thinks no group should be able to use the big theater more than one night a year.

"We have other clubs here," he said. "If we give them a second night, then every other club will want to get a second night."

And what about the rumor that the real reason the condo was denying the players a second night was money? That the condo board didn't want to pay for the lights and air conditioning in the theater?

Not true, King said.

"It's not a question of income," he said. "Just policy. We don't want to discriminate against the other clubs."

Al Price, the theater reviewer for *The Kings Point News*, has a different take on the situation.

"It's just a coverup of stupidity," he said.

The condo just signed up too many outside professional acts to perform in the theater, he said. Kings Point is a popular spot for seasoned performers who do the Catskills in the summer and Florida in the winter.

The condo theater, Price said, just got stretched too thin to accommodate the local performers.

"Sometimes the governing board forgets who they are working for," Price said.

The Players got more than 900 residents to sign a petition last month that asked the board to reconsider its decision.

Compromises have been in the air. A Sunday matinee. A second show in a smaller hall. But nothing has panned out yet. Well, almost nothing.

"We're going to allow them to hire an outside director," said the condo board's King.

Musical directors are harder to find in Kings Point than piano players, he explained.

And nonmusical directors, it seems, are still the easiest to find of all.

Boca Country Club pool duel: It's grandmas vs. kiddies
May 24, 1992

Fecal furor in full flower: Did diaper droppings pollute pool?

The search is on.

The scientists have put their pool water samples in incubators. The colonies are growing. The bacteria are multiplying.

The Boca Raton Country Club members are waiting.

C'mon, fecal matter!

Most people wouldn't root for the presence of you-know-what in their swimming pool. But things have been odd at the private club ever since a kiddie swim class invaded this haven for recumbent grandmas and grandpas.

Reports of gray-haired terrorism included splashing water at the kids. Others raised righteous indignation.

"We didn't buy into this place with the idea of making it into a summer camp," member Elaine Kace told a reporter.

But the club's managers held their ground. Yes, it is a private club, but the management owns the pool. And it has decided to allow the summer swimming program for infants and toddlers.

End of discussion? Not a chance.

The poolside commandos struck below the belt, summoning the Palm Beach County Health Unit inspectors to their club for water testing. That testing led to findings of bacteria in the water and the decision by health officials to close the pool for the weekend.

Undoubtedly, some members will hail the precautionary closing as a major victory, blame the bacteria on diapered kiddies and say they should learn swimming elsewhere.

They'll say the bacteria is an indication of fecal matter — that while these babies have been blowing bubbles and kicking their little Flintstone feet, they've been insidiously polluting the pool with their diapered droppings.

Covert bombing?

Somebody's got to get to the bottom of this.

That man is the Health Unit's Umesh Asrani.

And he is acting like a person who has stepped in something he wished he hadn't.

"There's no standard for swimming pool coliform," he said. "The chlorine residual assures the pathogenic bacteria will be killed."

In English, that means that even if there is a little bacteria there, the chlorine is going to kill it. Or, put another way, what's a little fecal matter among friends?

But fecal furor is in full flower.

The Health Unit's first samples were taken Wednesday and analyzed Friday. The deep water showed no coliform bacteria. The shallow end showed a "really low" reading, Asrani said.

But not all coliform bacteria is fecal matter.

"We have to do more testing," Asrani said.

So, inspectors returned for more testing. The results of that testing? Traces of bacteria, a two-day closing of the pool and another round of testing.

And what if this type of coliform is the fecal variety?

Does this answer the golden question? Are babies having bowel movements in the pool?

"No. You don't have to 'go' in the pool for it to show up," Asrani said. "There could just be residue — from adults as well as children."

Wait a minute. Adults could be the source of this? Is there any way to distinguish between kiddie and adult fecal bacteria?

"Not at all," Asrani said.

But are they as likely to pollute the pool?

"People don't seem to remember that there are a lot of older people who are incontinent, too," the Health Unit's Art Williams said.

I sense a JFK-styled mystery here. (How many shooters?) The science doesn't exist to make culprits of anyone. If the intention of the poolside commandos is to blame the kids, it won't work.

Not until the technology can tie the source of bacteria to traces of Huggies or Depends.

Berm abrasion: Cautionary tales of communal living

Men and their game start a Bellaggio brouhaha
March 26, 2010

Stodginess kills community's stickball team

Bellaggio, a sprawling active-adult community west of Lake Worth, got decidedly less active recently when the men who gather twice a week in the clubhouse parking lot were told they could no longer play stickball there.

For seven years, a group of mostly New York-area transplants has gathered in the parking lot on Tuesday and Thursday mornings to relive a game from their childhoods.

"When I was looking for a place to live," said Jack Koeppel, "we drove here and I saw guys playing stickball, and I said to my wife, 'This is where I want to live.' I signed up that day."

The few dozen men who play stickball had an informal agreement with their community, which painted a home plate for them in the parking lot and displayed their trophies in the clubhouse. Bellaggio's traveling squad, The Bellaggio Blue Diamonds, was last year's champ in the eight-community outdoor stickball league based in Wellington.

But things soured this year when a few of the homeowners whose property is within a foul-ball's distance of home plate complained about the noise and the occasional ball retrieval from their back yards.

"There's a clause in the regulations that says they're entitled to peace and quiet," said Alan Goldberg, the leader of the stickball group.

Goldberg and other players have been trying to work out an accommodation with the governing board and management. The players have offered to put up a screen behind home plate, or to find another spot in the community to play.

But stickball requires pavement for the bouncing ball, and the place best suited for the game is the big, nearly empty parking lot where they've been playing. It's a double if you hit the palm trees. A triple if you reach the light pole, and homer if the ball sails past the stop sign.

There are plenty of disputed calls, but no base running.

"If we had to run, we'd be dead by the end of the first inning," Neil Hecht said.

The men gathered that morning, after being told in advance that it would be the final day they'd be allowed to play in the parking lot.

But they never played, because when the property manager, Lynn Poirier, heard that a photographer and I were there, she stormed out of her office, striding across the parking lot with a determined gait.

Suddenly, they weren't men anymore, but little boys about to be yelled at by their mom.

And she was there to punish them for allowing their plight be heard outside the guard gates of their community.

"You're not playing today," Poirier told them.

The guys shuffled around home plate, not ready to go home, but not ready to wage a stickball rebellion. Then, one by one, they left.

Neil Hecht's wife arrived because she heard there was trouble at the stickball game, and wanted to make sure that her husband wasn't getting too worked up.

"This game is their life," Carole Hecht said. "He begs me to come down to Florida earlier every year so he can start playing stickball."

Cup of Joe stirs pot-load of controversy in Royal Palm Beach
April 26, 2002

Oh, trouble is a-brewin' in the condo's clubhouse

This is a condo dispute over a cup of instant coffee.

Yes, the police have been involved. The brandished weapon: a wooden cane. The feisty "victim": an 84-year-old woman.

Like many disputes of this nature, only fools wade in.

So here I go.

The clubhouse kitchen at Greenway Village South in Royal Palm Beach isn't locked — but it's rarely open. If it's card night or movie night in the clubhouse, then the kitchen is used. But during the day?

"If you want a cup of coffee, make it at home," said Lisa Aulita, who chairs the condo's board. "Why come to the clubhouse to make

Berm abrasion: Cautionary tales of communal living

coffee? We don't have a coffee klatch. That's not the kind of people we are."

So when fellow board member Mario Salazar emerged from the clubhouse kitchen late one morning with a cup of coffee in his hand, Aulita blasted him.

"He did not follow the rules and regulations," Aulita explained. "There has to be a certain order. We don't want anybody making coffee and leaving the electricity on."

The condo clubhouse burned down 10 years ago, and although it wasn't coffee-related, the kitchen should only be used with lots of supervision, Aulita said.

Salazar tried to explain. It's not like he was making a 10-course meal there.

He was using his cup, and his jar of Maxwell House instant decaffeinated coffee, which he had donated to the clubhouse.

"I used the water from the kitchen and the microwave," he said. "Everything else was mine. I didn't even use any of their sugar or cream, because I take my coffee black."

Aulita wasn't impressed.

"I told him, 'Mario, it doesn't make a hoot of difference whose coffee it is,' " she said.

The coffee debate played out in front of a condo employee and Florence Alpert, president of one of the four condo phases.

"They were humiliating me in front of the maintenance guy," Salazar said. "She said I threatened her with my cane and that I was swinging it all around. I would not do that. The only thing I did was slam the cane down on the table because I was mad."

Salazar, 57, uses the cane to help him walk.

"I wouldn't call him handicapped," Aulita said. "He walks like all of us, he has a little limp."

Alpert said he slammed the cane down hard and called Aulita a profane name. Both Salazar and Aulita agreed on the noun. There's a minor disparity in the modifying adjective.

"When he called me that," Aulita said, "for the first time in my life I put myself in the shoes of a woman who had been raped."

But wait, there's more.

Salazar said the real issue here is that he is gay, and the 84-year-old Aulita always finds a way to fight with him because of it.

"It took me over a year to get on the board," Salazar said, "while somebody else who was barely here a month got to be on the board."

Aulita said her gripes with Salazar have nothing to do with his sexual orientation.

"He wants to be president," she said, "but he doesn't have the caliber to be president."

The coffee incident spawned threats of lawsuits and an assault complaint made by Aulita against Salazar.

"The police didn't do anything," Salazar said. "They were laughing."

Aulita said she decided not to pursue charges against Salazar, instead opting for his public apology at a board meeting this month.

"He kind of whispered it," Alpert said. "You could barely hear it on the tape."

Alpert tries not to get as worked up as her friend Aulita about condo politics.

"This is our life," Alpert said. "It's tragically funny. You just have to laugh."

CHAPTER 4
New Yorkers
Refugees from a hallowed land

Where do New Yorkers flee? Palm Beach County, of course
Nov. 26, 1995

If Long Islanders are the dressing, we're in a pickle

If you've moved here from Long Island and are easily offended, let me recommend that this be the last sentence you read of today's column.

New Yorkers: Refugees from a hallowed land

OK, I had a feeling you wouldn't stop there, so I'm throwing in this sentence as a buffer. Still reading? I figured as much. Fine. But just remember that you've been warned.

The subject of today's column is an alarming story that appeared this month in *Newsday*, Long Island's biggest newspaper.

Long Island is apparently hemorrhaging Long Islanders, and the newspaper decided to find out where they are going.

So the paper dispatched a reporter to Boca Raton.

Good guess.

"Where do I go to find people from Long Island?" the reporter, Ken Moritsugu, asked me.

Moritsugu had just arrived and was calling from the Boca Raton Sheraton.

The answer, of course, was: "Anywhere."

Finding people from Long Island in Boca Raton has got to rank among the easiest assignments in American journalism.

The tougher question would be "I'm in Boca, where can I find people from Florida?"

Newsday did its own census and found that more than a third of Long Islanders who leave end up coming to Florida, and the most popular destination in the state is Palm Beach County.

And these aren't just retirees. No way. The census showed that nearly four out of five Long Islanders moving away were under 65.

Middle-aged working people. People who could dig deep roots here and remind us for decades, how even though they live here, things were much better in New York.

And for those who haven't figured it out yet, *Newsday's* story was like a billboard, announcing to Long Islanders that our county is the fleeing place.

The newspaper even went so far as to publish a quality-of-life comparison chart showing Palm Beach County vs. Long Island.

Naturally, we came out looking pretty good. Especially in the "annual snowfall" category.

Like I said, this is an alarming story.

You see, I'm of the opinion that we already have more than our fair share of former Long Islanders in Palm Beach County.

I should know. I'm one of them. And I've reached the conclusion that people like me are better appreciated in small doses.

Think of it as mayonnaise.

No mayonnaise, and you've got a bland sandwich. A nice smear of mayo, and you've got it made. Too much mayonnaise, and it can turn your stomach.

Boca's awash in mayo.

I suspect that one of the reasons Long Islanders are leaving Long Island is that there are too many Long Islanders there.

I can't blame them for wanting to spread out.

But I just wish more of them would avail themselves of the untapped areas of the country.

Our local pizza places have taken enough blame. It's time for Long Islanders to find new areas to complain about. Maybe Iowa can step in. Or Idaho. Someplace with a lot of room would be the best.

I heard about the *Newsday* story when one of my brothers called me from New York last week.

"You were in the paper," he said.

Then he started laughing.

"What did it say?" I asked.

"Something about people from Long Island being like cockroaches," he said. "It was a nice mention."

Ah, the cockroach theory. I think I formulated that one pre-mayo.

I got a copy of the story. It said:

"Frank Cerabino, a 40-year-old columnist with The Palm Beach Post *and himself a graduate of Bay Shore High School, has occasionally poked fun at 'the New Yorker infestation' of Florida — likening it to cockroaches."*

For the record, let me say that comment was taken in context. (I've always wanted to do that. I'm so sick of people who say embarrassing things and then try to wiggle out by claiming they were taken "out of context.")

Not me. I stand by the embarrassing things I say. If you don't like it, too bad.

I'm not sure why I feel that way. It might be because I'm from Long Island.

Just be thankful there aren't more like me around here. Although there may be real soon, as that *Newsday* story gets passed around

New Yorkers: Refugees from a hallowed land 41

Long Island during the bleak, gray time of year there.

So get ready. More waves of Long Islanders may be on the way.

Maybe we can do something. Maybe if we all face north and shout on the count of three.

One. Two. Three.

"HOLD THE MAYO!"

Our little-town blues melt away — when we earn political sway
Sept. 30, 2010

Florida's clout is up to you, New Yorkers!

We need to be nicer to New Yorkers.

Hey, stop your groaning. I'm serious. In fact, we ought to start an "I Love Ex-New York" campaign in Florida.

And it has nothing to do with the considerable contributions our former New Yorkers have made in the areas of deli-meat appreciation, competitive shopping and the adoption of the track suit as evening wear.

No, I'm just being practical.

Florida is poised to gain two extra congressional districts.

Instead of having 25 members in the U.S. House of Representatives, we'll have 27. And where will we be getting these two seats?

Start spreading the news — from New York.

The relative sizes of state delegations are determined by population, and every 10 years a reapportionment is made. Election Data Services just released a study that showed that the migration of New Yorkers to Florida would result in a shift of two congressional seats from New York to Florida.

Yes, if they can't make it there, they'll make it anywhere in Boynton Beach.

Sure, there's a downside.

The shift of seats would make Florida and New York tied for the third-largest state in Electoral College clout.

So Florida would have even more influence in presidential

elections.

Never a comforting thought.

It would also give the Republican-controlled state legislature two more gerrymandering opportunities. Even though registered Democrats outnumber Republicans in Florida, state lawmakers have drawn congressional districts that are held by 15 Republicans in the existing 25 districts.

Now, they'll have two more seats to carve out for friends, who will undoubtedly try to hop on the Washington gravy train by campaigning for smaller government.

But I prefer to look at the bright side. We need former New Yorkers.

They allow the Florida Marlins to have a respectable attendance for at least nine home games every season. And they're extremely helpful when it comes to offering a better way to do almost anything.

"Back in New York, we (insert superior method here)..."

And so it's critical that we nurture them.

That's because the congressional seat shift isn't final yet.

Election Data Services pointed out that Florida might only gain one seat, instead of two, if the expected migration from New York to Florida is slightly less than projected.

How much less? About 85,000 people. So if 85,000 New Yorkers either decided to stay put or move from Florida back to New York, we might not pick up that second seat.

So let's spread the love to transplanted New Yorkers for the rest of the year.

If they cut in front of you in line – OK, let me rephrase that – when they cut in front of you in line, just smile. And never argue about the pizza.

"Yes, it's all terrible here," you should say, and then add helpfully, "So what did the Yankees do today?"

Some future congressman from Florida will thank you.

New Yorkers: Refugees from a hallowed land

Not only do we get Long Islanders — now we get their number, too (almost)
Dec. 1, 1995

New area code puts Long Island just a digit away

It's time to start rounding up suspects.

Who did this to us? Who's the wise guy here? I'm talking about that new area code we're getting. 561.

Somebody's got a sick sense of humor in the phone company.

I suspect it's that woman with the recorded voice. The Ironic Woman. You know the one I'm talking about. She's the one you hear when you dial wrong.

First, she punishes you by rattling every dental appliance in your head with those three ear-piercing tones.

Then she says mockingly, "If you'd like to make a call, . . ."

Of course "I'd like to make a call." That's why I have a phone in my hand. I'm not dialing because "I'd like to make toast."

I figure it must be her or someone just like her at the phone company who came up with the new area code we're getting in April.

I'm not questioning the fact that we need a new number. I believe the phone company when it says our area's becoming overwhelmed by all the numbers being glommed by pagers and cellular phones. (I can remember the good old days, when only drug dealers and bail bondsmen had pagers and cell phones.)

But what I question is the number itself — 561.

Before I explain, let me give you my credentials. I'm a graduate of the Louis Farrakhan School of Conspiracy Theories (White Devil Campus), with a major in Placing Incredible Importance on Seemingly Innocuous Numbers and Letters.

So, I've given this quite a bit of thought. And despite my schooling, I've concluded that, for once, the Masons aren't to blame for this.

No, it's much simpler than that. Somebody at the phone company is playing a joke on us.

Before the new numbers were announced this week, I had always agreed with columnist Calvin Trillin's theory on area codes. Trillin suspected that the phone company employed someone he called The Far Away Man, whose job it was to devise area codes in such a way that a one-number slip would have callers dialing clear across the country from their intended number.

Trillin's theory explained why we have a 407 area code here. The two most similar area codes to ours — 406 and 307 — belong to Montana and Wyoming, respectively.

You've got to wonder how many people dialed wrong, thinking they were going to speak to their dear Aunt Gladys at Century Village, and hooked up, instead, with a Marlboro Man at 5 a.m., his time.

For some reason, the phone company must have ignored The Far Away Man's recommendation for our new area code. Or perhaps, The Far Away Man is nearing retirement age, and so he has begun to pass the area-code baton to his successor.

The Ironic Woman.

Because this is surely ironic.

We're getting Long Island's area code. Not only do we get Long Islanders, but now we get their area code too.

Or about as close as you can get to it.

Long Island: 516.

Us: 561.

Phone company: Ha, ha, ha.

You see the humor here? Soon, when you dial incorrectly, you'll have no way of knowing it.

At least when you got a Marlboro Man, you knew something was wrong, right off the bat. You knew that your connection to condo land had gone astray, or you wouldn't have been hearing all that background bleating of freshly branded cattle.

It was a quick hang up when The Far Away Man was in charge. But with this new area code, who knows how long these errant conversations might go on.

There's a good chance that there will be Long Island accents on both ends of the phone. It could take a good five minutes before you realize that the person you're talking to isn't in Delray or Boynton, but is in some Long Island garden spot such as Speonk, Yaphank or the ever-whimsical Shirley.

(As in, "I got caught for speeding in Shirley.")

I imagine that in lieu of pay raises at the phone company next year, employees will be offered a chance to listen in on these misguided calls.

"Joey, is that you?"

"Whah?"

"Haah?"

"Joey who?"

"Whah?"

"Donna?"

"Haah?"

"Whah?"

"You got the wrong number!"

"No, you got the wrong number!"

"Haah?"

"Whah?"

Former New Yorkers are our signature human resource
Feb. 25, 2009

Let's find a way to make New Yorkers feel more at home

We're hemorrhaging New Yorkers.

I know, I know. Doesn't seem possible. But the numbers don't lie. The Associated Press compared Florida driver license applications from 2003 and 2008 and discovered that the state has experienced a 40 percent decline in new residents from New York, New Jersey and Pennsylvania over that five-year period.

This is especially significant for Palm Beach County, which leads the state in New York refugees and has been imbued with a sixth-borough *je ne sais quoi* that now stands to be in the throes of a steep decline.

Of course, this would be a shame. For we former New Yorkers are the salt of the earth, a quiet, unassuming lot of gentle souls who tread softly upon this once-savage land, gracing it with our lilting voices, our "you first" social impulses, and the necessary repudiation of Miracle Whip as a palatable sandwich condiment.

OK, well, maybe I laid that on a little thick. And maybe you think that fewer New Yorkers is good news.

But you shouldn't.

Florida's in a recession now, and we here in Palm Beach County need to hang on to our assets. And for us that means hanging on to former New Yorkers, whether we like them or not.

For there are no bigger assets than former New Yorkers.

I'm not just talking about me. Former New Yorkers are our signature human resource. Without them, we'd be a Trump-less backwater, an oceanfront Bradenton, a place where full-contact shopping, recreational medical treatment and Liza Minnelli tickets would be unattainable fantasies.

So here's my suggestion: We've got to suck it up for the sake of our economy and find a way to make Palm Beach County feel more like home to New Yorkers.

I can hear you whining that we're already way too much like New York, and what we need to do is accelerate the retreat of New Yorkers by turning the Kravis Center into an "opry" house or committing some other similar act of egregious effrontery.

But remember, this is about our survival. We need to find a way to bring New Yorkers back, even if that might mean doing something unconventional, even uncomfortable, for the rest of us.

Here are three changes we can make now:

Start spreading the news

For some reason, New Yorkers never get tired of hearing the song *New York, New York*, which sometimes devolves into a sloppy kick-line finale, especially when combined with the overconsumption of alcoholic beverages.

Yes, I know this song is more than annoying. But it's played at the end of every New York Yankees game, which makes it practically a religious observance.

So to make New Yorkers feel more welcome here, the song should be played at the conclusion of all public meetings, at closing time at the malls and repeatedly during NewYorkFest.

SunFest? Fuhgeddaboudit

The outdoor music festival called SunFest will be renamed

NewYorkFest.

The five-day event still will be held on Flagler Drive in West Palm Beach, but it now will be controlled by a consortium of trash haulers, labor unions and Italian bread distributors.

Motor sports a no-no

Nothing says Alabama more than motor sports. New Yorkers, who believe that civilization ends somewhere near Exit 3 on the New Jersey Turnpike, need to be reassured that there are few, if any, actual Southerners in Palm Beach County.

Unfortunately, the Palm Beach International Raceway west of Jupiter is a physical reminder that Palm Beach County has a geographical and cultural foothold in the South.

For the public good, the track needs to be turned into an enormous Loehmann's.

CHAPTER 5

Car troubles
Real people in a wheel jam

Two cars, kids of all ages, and a gun equals strange road rage
September 18, 1996

There's nothing like the fury of a mooned mom

Another cautionary tale from Interstate 95.

Our central character today — and a real character, to boot — is Josh Lucias, a mild-mannered 22-year-old lawn equipment mechanic. This is his story.

Josh was on a mission of mercy on a weekend afternoon, helping his friend, Cosmo, move into a new apartment in Lantana. The chums were driving from Josh's home in Plantation. By noon, they were northbound on I-95 in a rented U-Haul truck, Cosmo behind the wheel, Josh in the passenger seat.

As they passed the Glades Road interchange in Boca Raton, Cosmo shouted: "That lady just cut me off!"

That lady was Montrose Herbert, 33, who happened to not only have three kids in her car, ages 11, 8 and 5, but also a loaded 9mm handgun.

Josh didn't know about the gun at the time. He didn't see the kids, either.

"I wasn't paying attention," he said. "My friend was the guy who was driving. I didn't even know he got cut off."

But it must have been an impressive maneuver, because Cosmo was miffed.

Common traffic etiquette on I-95 called for an inaudible mutter, at the least, to a one-finger salute, at the most.

But Cosmo thought this warranted more.

"Moon her," he told his friend.

So as Cosmo maneuvered the U-Haul into proper mooning position, Josh climbed up on the seat, dropped his drawers, and as he so quaintly put it, "left a print on the glass."

It wasn't something he weighed in his mind.

He'd mooned before.

"Doesn't everybody moon from the limo during prom night?" he asked.

Maybe that was the first time. But this would be the last. It was right about the time Josh was putting his southern extremity back in his trousers when he noticed the gun.

"It was aimed right at me," Josh said.

The woman in the Caddy shot and missed. Everything. Even the truck.

"She must be a lousy shot," Josh said.

Even so, Cosmo decided it would be best not to give her another try. So the U-Haul hauled with the Cadillac in pursuit.

Just another Sunday afternoon on I-95: a mooner trying to flee a gun-toting mom.

"Cosmo just made sure we stayed in front of her car," Josh said.

The chase was a four-exit affair, ending at Atlantic Avenue in Delray Beach, when Herbert got off the interstate.

Josh and Cosmo figured they were safe. Three hours later, after unloading the truck in Lantana, they were back on I-95 making the return trip to Plantation.

If what happened next had happened in a movie, you wouldn't believe it.

Once again, as they cruised past Boca Raton, they chanced upon the woman with the 9mm gun in the Cadillac. This time they were both heading south.

And Herbert, who still had some ammo left, decided she was still angry enough to put a crater in the moon man.

She fired at the U-Haul again, and the chase, once again, was on.

"I figured somebody would stop us," Josh said. "We were weaving in and out of traffic in this U-Haul with this wild lady after us."

The U-Haul got off the highway at the Sunrise Boulevard exit in Fort Lauderdale. The Caddy followed. When they got stopped at a light, the woman pulled a 2-by-4 piece of wood out of her trunk and began hitting the U-Haul with it.

"We've got to find some cops," Josh said. "This lady's nuts."

After they got rolling again, Cosmo spotted some Plantation officers at a gas station. He pulled in. The woman was right behind.

"At first, I was happy," Josh said. "The Plantation cops thought it was pretty funny. Then the Florida Highway Patrol cop showed up and it wasn't funny anymore.

"He said because I took my pants down in front of children, it was a felony."

The woman in the Cadillac was also in trouble, charged with aggravated assault and unsafe storage of a firearm — which she left loaded in the car with her unattended kids when she ran out to the U-Haul at the end of the chase.

Josh ended up in the Palm Beach County Jail from Sunday night to Tuesday afternoon, when the charge against him was lowered to a misdemeanor.

Will he be doing any more drive-by moonings on I-95?

"I don't think so," he said.

Car sera sera? Verbal volleys launched from English-only emails
October 10, 2007

Spanish-American war breaks out on car commercials

Earl Stewart needs to stop advertising in Spanish.

The North Palm Beach car dealer should realize that Japanese cars ought to be sold in English. It's simply un-American to speak Spanish on an English-language TV station when advertising Toyotas.

Stewart has a lot of chutzpah to presume he has *carte blanche* with the language of his ads.

Did George Washington rout the British at Yorktown for nothing? No, he did it (with the help of the French) so that we could all speak English, our beloved mother tongue.

How dare this car dealer tarnish the memory of our Founding Fathers with his Spanish language commercials with English subtitles at a time when we're going *mano a mano* with terrorists.

This is America. We don't need to learn anybody's language but our own.

Capice?

If you want to sell a Solara, do it in English.

Our American ears should not be exposed to any strange-sounding words, especially ones in the language of the designated scapegoats for the upcoming election year.

We can't be building a wall to keep Spanish speakers out of the country while welcoming the ones already here as customers.

Stewart needs to wake up and smell the venti-sized latte.

This is no time for a *laissez faire* attitude to our language.

His big tent approach has put us all in deep kimchi.

Stewart's ads were the fodder for a national news story on CNN, activating a new wave of patriots who emerged from their bunkers to sound the alarm. So we here in Palm Beach County may be getting the reputation of being soft on language, when we could be the *creme de la creme* of English defenders.

"An atrocity has occurred against America," one uber-patriot

Car troubles: Real people in a wheel jam

e-mailer wrote me this week in complaint about Stewart.

"Forward this to EVERY American you know," the patriot continued.

Even the traitors?

See what Stewart has started? You stimulate these English-only people, and you're one step away from activating United Nations conspiracy buffs and half the field of any Republican primary.

"This is a slippery slope we're headed for," the e-mail continued. "If we don't stop this type of anti-American behavior, it may just become commonplace to see English speaking television channels airing their programs in Spanish, Chinese or some other foreign language."

You start speaking Chinese, and the next thing you know they'll think that American box stores should sell their cheap tchotchkes. That'll be the day!

(You'll get my lead-based toy when you pry it from my cold, dead fingers.)

It's time we defend the status quo against anybody who doesn't revere the only language we thought we'd ever need to know.

Stewart has his reasons for advertising in Spanish on English language TV:

Toyotas are popular with Hispanics. Advertising on Miami-based Spanish-language TV is far more costly. And most Hispanic customers are bilingual, tending to watch English-language TV anyway.

"I want to speak in their native tongue as a matter of respect to them," Stewart said. "I'm just trying to sell a few more cars."

But at the cost of angering the language purists who insist on a quid pro quo between devotion to English and living in the land of freedom.

Plus, Stewart's Spanish-language commercial is an affront to the Spanish language, too.

"I memorized what I had to say and I had cue cards," he said, "but it still took me 25 takes."

All he gets out of it is more business, and an open-minded approach in close-minded times.

Alert every American. *Pronto.*

Frank's personal sacrifice is taken to lower (road) levels
January 31, 1996

Kowal's skills need a road test first; I'll watch minivan

It's time for sensible people to take charge here.

I'm talking about the debacle over contract negotiations with the woman picked to be the next Palm Beach County schools superintendent. What really has people upset isn't that Joan Kowal is holding out for more money from local taxpayers.

It's that she wants us to buy her a minivan, a 1996 Chrysler Town & Country minivan. She was that specific. She wants the Chrysler.

I guess she thought we'd counter with something like, "How 'bout a Chevy Astro?"

But instead, some of the locals have countered with indignation. Some are even saying we should break off negotiations with Kowal. And County Commissioner Karen Marcus, usually a level-headed sort, has already branded Kowal as the Minivan Lady.

I say we all calm down.

Kowal just made a mistake. A bad one.

Let's not crucify her — just yet. Let's see if we can work this out like rational people.

I've got a bad feeling that if we let Kowal slip away, we're going to suddenly end up with Maria Sachs on the next short list of school superintendents, now that Maria's husband can't wangle a judgeship for her.

So I've got a plan to smooth things out with Kowal, a plan that I think will satisfy the taxpayers as well as her.

Joan, we're just not buying you a minivan. At least, not right away.

Why does Kowal need a minivan?

First of all, Kowal's got no kids. It may even be against the law to own a minivan without children.

(Note to editors: Can somebody check that out so I don't look like a complete fool in the morning paper? Thanks.)

Secondly, who can afford to buy a new minivan these days?

I can't. And probably neither can you. They've become suburban assault vehicles, costing about $30,000. Clearly, Kowal can get by with something a little smaller.

I think we should give her a car. After all, as the head of an institution that will mold our county's future, she deserves a car of her own from us.

And I've got just the car for her.

My car.

Not that I want to get rid of it. It's only got 124,000 miles on it.

But I'm willing to make a sacrifice for the common good if it means getting us through this rocky contract negotiation period.

And my 1989 Toyota Corolla is just the car for Kowal.

She needs a public relations boost. She has gotten off on the wrong foot, gaining a reputation as a money-grubber before she even gets here.

But put her behind the wheel of my Corolla and people will have only sympathy for her.

In fact, if we give her my car, it might not even be considered a perk.

There she'll be, sweating profusely (the air conditioner's been broken for two years) as she pulls up to work. Everybody in the Taj Majal will know it's her (because of the loud muffler announcing her arrival) as she peers behind the cracked windshield and petrified tree sap in a vehicle whose heavily oxidized paint job gets a lighter shade of red every year from the sun.

I love my car, learning over the years to grow attached to its trick windows, temperamental turn-signal, and get-up-and-go that got up and went.

Naturally, it will be a sacrifice for me to give it up. Which brings me to the second part of my plan.

The school board should buy me the Chrysler minivan. I've got kids. I can fill that sucker in a heartbeat.

And it'll be a wise investment on the county's part. Here's how:

You give me the minivan for, say, two years. That'll be enough time to know whether Kowal's a keeper or not.

Tell her right up front, "Cerabino's getting your van for now, but you can have it in a couple of years if we think you're doing a good job."

The wisdom of this move is awesome.

If you give the van to Kowal right away, she could just turn out to be a lousy supe, last a year, and scram with the van. But by giving it to me, you know it's in the hands of a guy who's going nowhere.

Heck, I don't even go to lunch. You know I'll be here in two years to turn over the keys.

Kowal, meanwhile, will be a woman possessed in those first two years, desperately trying to work hard so she can graduate from my public-relations-friendly Toyota to the minivan she has always wanted.

Meanwhile, the school board gets the added benefit of muzzling me for two whole years. I won't be able to write a word about their new hire, Kowal.

That's because as long as I'm driving the minivan, I'll have a conflict of interest. She'll have a two-year honeymoon from getting Cerabinoed.

And what superintendent wouldn't love to begin a job with the security of knowing that a wisenheimer like me would have to keep his big mouth shut. It's what county commissioners like to call "a win-win situation."

Of course, I'll really miss my Corolla. But being a team player is what I'm all about.

So, the Corolla's waiting, Joan. As for the minivan, I like it forest green. I hope that's OK with you.

WHAT'S THE DIFFERENCE?
Exterior touches

The Chrysler minivan: Sliding glass doors on both sides.

The Cerabino Corolla: Dents on both sides from falling driveway basketball pole and backboard.

Bags

The Chrysler minivan: Air bags for both front seats.

The Cerabino Corolla: Fast-food bags under both front seats.

Console features:

The Chrysler minivan: Compass, mini-trip computer.

The Cerabino Corolla: About three bucks worth of loose change lost and jangling inside emergency brake slot.

Car troubles: Real people in a wheel jam

Frank stands proudly at the side of his 1989 Toyota Corolla

Windshield features

The Chrysler minivan: Wiper de-icers, solar control glass.

The Cerabino Corolla: Cracked glass from following gravel truck too closely on I-95.

Road Test

As you will see, Frank Cerabino's 1989 Toyota Corolla stacks up favorably against the 1996 Chrysler Town & Country minivan. In measuring the comparisons, refer to the following key of symbols:

(*) ... special instructions necessary to accomplish this task

(#) ... not advisable during the warm-weather months

((CT)) ... take off shirt

(%) ... taking a few Tylenols makes it better

Anti-theft features

The Chrysler minivan: Security alarm; central locking.

The Cerabino Corolla: None needed. You can park it in a bad neighborhood with the windows open and the keys in the ignition and nobody will try to steal it.

Air conditioning

The Chrysler minivan: Dual zone temperature control.

The Cerabino Corolla: Broken. Roll down windows. (*) Or seek relief in other ways. ((CT))

Special sound features

The Chrysler minivan: Rear floor silencer to reduce exterior noise.

The Cerabino Corolla: Loud muffler.(%) When it gets too awful, roll up windows. (*) (#)

Stereo

The Chrysler minivan: AM/FM with cassette, CD, equalizer, and 10 speakers.

The Cerabino Corolla: To hear it on road, windows must be rolled up. (#) If you really want to listen during that time, consider other measures. ((CT))

Window features

The Chrysler minivan: Power controls, with driver 'one-touch' capability.

The Cerabino Corolla: Manual, with broken handle on front passenger side, and customized 'two-hand-yank-on-glass' system to adjust driver's window. (%)

Jupiter Island drives by Death Race 2000 rules: Hit a worker and keep going

August 04, 2006

Make driver apologize for hitting man? That's rich

I hope we've learned something from James Crews.

Crews, 46, was the construction worker hit by an elderly socialite who was driving to the Jupiter Island Club for an afternoon of card-playing earlier this year. Very bad behavior.

No, not for Jane Choate, the 87-year-old socialite, who according to a witness, struck the flagman with her Lexus as he was directing traffic on South Beach Road on Jupiter Island, then yelled something to him before hitting him a second time with her car and continuing on to the club.

This is what people are supposed to do on Jupiter Island. Go to the club to play cards. Construction workers should be invisible and quiet.

The bad actor in this story is clearly Crews, who had the nerve to track Choate down at the club, call the police and think that she should be charged with something as inconvenient as leaving the scene of an accident, a felony.

Fortunately, the island police didn't let all this law-and-order business get in the way of good manners. The officer at the scene didn't arrest her, and more important, allowed her to finish playing her game of bridge on that January afternoon.

It's a wonder all that fuss didn't cause the poor woman to ruin the day by trumping her partner's trick or blowing a grand slam.

This week, Choate's case was disposed of in court with probation, community service and an order to apologize — something she declined to do in court.

Can't blame her. She's probably still angry about being interrupted at the club.

To make matters worse, Crews had the poor taste to point out that if the tables were turned, if he had struck her, and then continued on to a lunch at Wendy's, the officer might not have allowed him to finish his burger and make an appointment to talk about the matter at his convenience.

Well, of course not. The rules of etiquette do not apply to workers on Jupiter Island, Palm Beach, Manalapan, or any similarly situated community of wealth.

Doesn't everybody know that?

Maybe not. So on behalf of all the other potential James Crewses out there, here are the rules:

Rule No. 1: Don't scream.

Yes, we know you're in pain. But chances are that the sight of blood or the exposed bone already makes that clear. So hush up. People treasure their quiet time here, and chances are, all that howling and yelping you'd do would just end up violating a local noise ordinance.

Just dust yourself off and get back to work.

Rule No. 2: Don't call the police.

They're busy hassling other nonresidents who have the nerve to be in town in anything other than a service vehicle. If they come out to take your report, it just means you'll get less work done that day, which means you'll have to remain in town longer than necessary. Not good.

Just dust yourself off and get back to work.

Rule No. 3: Don't be rude to the resident who injured you.

Maybe they're having a tough investment day. If they stop to yell at you for slowing them down, just pop any bones back inside your body, nod politely, and apologize for any inconvenience you might have caused.

Then dust yourself off and get back to work.

Rule No. 4: Offer your services.

If the resident who injures you doesn't decide to drive off right away, don't imagine that the reason is to apologize or check on your welfare.

Assume, instead, that you are being given an opportunity to check for the damage you did to the vehicle. If your shirt isn't excessively bloody, you can use it to buff up the paint job and scoop out any bits of flesh, cartilage or bone that may be stuck in the nooks and crannies of the car's grille.

Then dust yourself off and get back to work.

Little Red Corvette a parting shot for university president
February 28, 2003

Let's back off on Catanese: It's not like he got a new Jag

An open letter from Dr. Anthony Catanese:

Dear students, faculty members and all the fine people in the Florida Atlantic University and Boca Raton communities:

Not a day goes by when I don't think about the wonderful years I spent as president of FAU. Knowing you all has been a gift I shall never forget, a gift more precious than any parting gift a dynamic university president might receive from an understandably grateful school foundation.

More precious than say, a new red Corvette, which, by the way, drives great. Thanks for asking.

I know you may have read some scurrilous newspaper reports about my Corvette. These reports might lead you to believe that the school's fund-raising group laundered $42,000 through my dear wife, Sara, so I could purchase this car without it appearing to be bought with tax-deductible donor dollars.

I can't tell you how much this has hurt Sara. Just because she isn't a licensed interior decorator is no reason to assume that she couldn't legitimately be paid 40-large as a decoration consultant on her own home.

She's a whiz at decorating. Trust me on this. Why, just the other day, I got in the Corvette, and she had put one of those neat little dream-catcher thingies on the rear-view mirror.

I know some people might think that a parting gift of a Corvette might be a little excessive for a president of a public university who was already making $191,000 a year, with a $20,000 annual housing allowance and a leased Cadillac.

But it's so hard to find the right gift these days. Especially for a person like me.

I don't need any more plaques or Cross pens. And cash is so ... so impersonal.

And besides, it's not like I'm the only school head around here to make off with a car.

Just last week, Amelia Ostrosky, the former principal of the Dreyfoos School of the Arts in West Palm Beach, got a Jaguar. A Jaguar!

Now, that's a fishy case.

She sues the school board over getting moved from Dreyfoos, gets a chunk of change in a settlement, and then the Dreyfoos foundation raffles off a car and — get this — Ostrosky wins it.

Yeah, right. And in other news, Frank Brogan didn't have the FAU job sewn up from the get-go.

C'mon, people. Wake up and smell the Corinthian leather.

Why aren't people focusing more on the Dreyfoos Jaguar than the

FAU Corvette?

Take some pity on me.

I didn't even get to stick around long enough to enjoy the $3 million presidential palace built for me at FAU. That place is so regal, if it was in Iraq, we'd bomb it.

And Brogan, my FAU successor, finagled a compensation package worth a heart-stopping $368,000 a year! I would have stayed at FAU for that kind of jack.

Instead, I'm up here running this little collegiate cul-de-sac in Melbourne. Do you know what it's like going from Boca Raton to Melbourne?

I'll put it this way: When you order sushi in Melbourne, you check for fish hooks.

So, it saddens me to see what has become of my legacy at FAU. The Board of Trustees is at war with the Foundation. Door locks have been changed. And everybody's clamming up on the advice of their attorneys.

All over my red Corvette, which, by the way, drives great. Thanks for asking.

The justice vs. just us world of privileged lifestyles
September 22, 1993

Get-away car was a Rolls, hideout was condo tower

I'm a sucker for any cop story involving a medium-speed chase of a fleeing oil company executive driving a Rolls-Royce.

All too often, the local constabulary is relegated to pursuing the young and the restless. They're mostly a penniless bunch who can drive fast but lack the means, power and worldliness to turn a police chase into a work of art. So it's very refreshing to get an artful medium-speed chase of a 64-year-old captain of industry driving a Rolls.

One that has more to do with the Forbes 500 than the Indy 500.

Our star is Charles R. Brown, the owner of a Riviera Beach oil company and a man who seemed to be a quart low on patience one night.

Brown wanted to make a right turn on red so bad that he beeped, bumped and finally crashed his Rolls into the back of a Mercury Cougar, jolting the car into the middle of a Singer Island intersection.

All despite the driver of the Cougar trying to point out a traffic sign that said: No turn on red.

If only a cop were there, you might say.

Well, this was even better. The guy in the Cougar was Lake Park Police Chief Jeff Lindskoog, off-duty and in civilian clothes.

"He was damaging my car," Lindskoog said. "I did what any citizen would do — try to make sure he didn't get away with it."

So the chief began his medium-speed chase, content to follow the Rolls until it stopped.

Justice seemed to be close at hand.

But wait! Brown drove home, turning into the 43-story Tiara Condominium, a veritable Singer Island nation-state. A sanctuary with its own security force and its own notion of law and order.

A place where justice yields to just us.

Bad news for Lindskoog, who flashed his Lake Park badge at the gate and told the guard to call the Riviera Beach police to the condo.

Instead, the gate guard called a roving security guard. And pretty soon, it was the police chief who was confronted in the parking garage.

"I told them, 'I'm a police officer and this guy hit my car,'" Lindskoog said. "I didn't want him to disappear. But the security guard told me I was on private property and I would have to leave."

Lindskoog didn't want to leave until a Riviera Beach officer could arrive and determine whether Brown should be given a sobriety test.

"If it was in my jurisdiction, I would have given him the test," Lindskoog said.

But security chief William Simpson said his guards acted correctly in shooing the chief.

"He flashed a badge, but you don't know who he is," Simpson said. "And he shouldn't have conducted himself that way. He was rude."

Lindskoog drove up the street, called the Riviera Beach police and returned to the Tiara with a city officer.

Brown's car was still in the garage. But Brown wasn't. Lindskoog and officer Donald Million went to Brown's 39th floor apartment.

"While knocking on the door we could hear someone leaning up against the door and looking out the peep hole," Million wrote.

Police knew Brown was there because he had the gumption to call 911 to complain.

"There's somebody trying to get into this apartment," Brown told the dispatcher.

"Do you know who it is?" she asked.

"No."

"Did you ask?"

"No," he said. "They're beating on the door."

The dispatcher radioed units to respond to a break-in at Brown's condo. But when Million heard it, he stopped her, saying that he was the person at Brown's door.

"We need you to go to the door," the dispatcher told Brown. "That's the police."

"OK," he said.

But he didn't. And Million got tired of waiting.

"Tell him to come downstairs or I'm towing his Rolls-Royce," he later told the dispatcher.

And he did — a fitting, if not legally sufficient, bit of creative law enforcement.

The officer wrote up Brown for aggravated battery with a motor vehicle, but the state attorney's office reduced the charge to a few misdemeanors, including criminal mischief.

A wonderful performance all the way around.

A dogged police chief. Condo guards destined for fat Christmas bonuses. A brassy 911 call that the hoi polloi lacks the nerve to make. Some tow-truck justice. And a sobering lesson in the sovereign-immunity theory of condo living.

"We're here to protect the interests of the people here," security chief Simpson said.

Bravo. Well played. Everyone take a bow.

It's only in the monied version of the car-chase caper that you get such an entertainingly fuzzy distinction between the hunter and hunted.

CHAPTER 6
Palm Beach
"An island off the coast of the United States"

I'm in cahoots with the Count
March 1, 1996

Duke seeks SWIM
(A single, wealthy island matron)

One of the great joys of being a columnist in this area is that I occasionally hear from people like Henry Randmark.

"I'm a count from Denmark," Randmark explains. "And if this works out, I won't forget you, Frank." Then he adds, significantly, "This is not a deal for peanuts."

Suddenly, it seems, I'm in cahoots with the Count. A count is counting on me.

After a couple minutes of conversation, I've somehow become the guy who's supposed to find a woman for his buddy, a character who goes by the name His Royal Highness, Prince Reinhard of Saxony, Duke of Saxony.

"Looks are not important," the Count says. "It's strictly a business deal. She has to have a lot of money."

Naturally, the Count has come to sniff around Palm Beach for action.

"I've stayed at The Breakers many times," he says. "And I know there are a lot of reputable women in Palm Beach who are dripping with money."

The Duke needs some of it to drip on him.

I've always been a sucker for a good sob story. But it's hard keeping a straight face as the Count relates the sad tale of his pal, His Royal Highness, who is down to his last "small mansion" on the German coast.

"Since his wife died three years ago, he's been living off a small pension," the Count explains. "It makes him live like an average person, and he's not an average person. He comes from a family that used to have hundreds of castles."

And his bachelor pad in Hamburg — only a 2-bed, 1-bath. Imagine that!

Naturally, I'm beside myself in grief by now. Just tell me, Count, what can I do? What can I do?

The Count gets right to the point.

"Find him a woman, somebody who's got at least a few million," he says.

But what does she get out of the deal?

"She gets the royal title," he says. "She'd be both the Princess of Saxony and the Duchess of Saxony. And her children would be princes and princesses."

And how old's the Duke?

"Fifty."

And will his wife have to . . . you know . . . will she have to do anything else for, or with, the Duke?

"No," the Count says. "It's pure business. He's not looking for love. There are already a thousand women who want that. He just wants the money.

Officially, they would have to live together, but unofficially, they wouldn't."

So it begins and ends with money.

"And there shouldn't be any scandals, or a criminal record in her past, either," The Count says. "He's not looking for a hooker."

Heavens no. Sounds like he's just looking for a crazy person with money.

What exactly does the woman get out of this deal?

"She will get the noblest title in Europe," the Count says. "If you go some places with the royal crown on your card, all sorts of doors will open."

Well, you're in the right place, Count. If anybody's prone to do this, they're probably right here in Palm Beach. Where else have you tried chumming for women?

"I started in Switzerland and Austria," the Count says. "There were

Palm Beach: "An island off the coast of the United States" 65

a couple of possibilities there. One of them didn't have the money, and the other one did have the money, but her reputation was very bad. Then I went to New York."

New York didn't work out too well, either.

The Count landed a big write-up for his pal in a magazine called *Romantic Times*. But so far, he says, it has only landed him bites from American commoners who don't have the kind of coin the Duke has in mind.

"They're average people," the Count says. "Not Rockefellers, or Madonna or Joan Collins."

Suppose this woman is looking for more than a business deal? Suppose the Duke floats her boat?

"If there's romance, it will be something that happens afterward," the Count says.

No touching the merchandise, ladies. The lawyer signs the deal, you turn over your money, and then take things from there.

I told the Count I would see what I can do.

I'm hoping it works out. I can imagine the grateful Duke calling me up from the German starter-castle he would be able to buy since glomming the money from his new wife.

"What can I do for you?" he would ask me. "Would you like me to bestow a title on you?"

"No," I would say. "I already have one. I'm widely known around here as a Royal Pain in the . . ."

To cops, he's the devil in a blue-sequined dress
July 26, 1995

A real drag: Palm Beacher's free defense

Neil Cargile doesn't mind my writing about his drunken-driving arrest on Palm Beach.

The 67-year-old town resident doesn't even mind my mentioning what he was wearing that night. A red-sequined minidress.

Big deal. The mining company executive's been showing up in public places wearing women's clothes for decades.

"After all the years, you collect a lot of sequined dresses," Cargile said.

But what's embarrassing to him is his lawyer.

A public defender. Don't mention that, he said.

It doesn't look right when Palm Beach executives have a lawyer whose purpose is to provide legal help for the poor.

"I dumped every penny I've got in a mining operation in Guyana," Cargile said. "To get one of these cases defended by somebody that's worthwhile is expensive."

So we taxpayers are helping Cargile out.

We're giving him the legal help he needs to beat a drunken-driving charge that, according to Cargile, is simply the product of a police officer who didn't like the looks of a 6-foot, 182-pound man dressed up as "SheNeil."

Just skip the lawyer business, Cargile said. Nobody cares who gets a public defender, anyway.

I try to explain to him that it's interesting when Palm Beach CEOs get public defenders. But he doesn't seem interested.

"I keep a low profile in Palm Beach," he said. "Except for the women's clothes."

Even he laughs at that.

What about the women's clothes?

"I just have a great time doing it," he said. "I usually wear them when I go out on Friday and Saturday nights."

Cargile, who grew up among the privileged class in Nashville, has had an interesting life. Two marriages, three kids and a reputation as a daredevil airplane pilot.

This year, *New Yorker* magazine ran a long profile of him. The writer of the piece met Cargile in Manhattan for lunch at Tavern on the Green. Cargile, according to the piece, showed up at the elegant restaurant dressed in a man's blazer and shirt, along with a microminiskirt, pantyhose and high heels.

"I thought I'd come half and half," he told the writer.

Cargile talks like a tough guy and is not beyond hinting at physical harm to those who wise off to him.

He uses the men's room when he's dressed as "SheNeil." That's because even with the wigs, makeup, dresses and support garments, he's not trying to fool anybody. He knows he still looks like a man.

"Too much muscle," he said.

And besides, he said, he doesn't want to deal with the reaction women might have if he walked into a women's restroom.

"I'd rather put up with the men," he said.

Cargile doesn't act like a guy who puts up with much. He's got the kind of bravado you'd expect from an international businessman and former Navy pilot.

"Most people know me where I go around here," he said. "The bartenders tell people I'm all right."

He's just different. It began when he showed up at a Halloween charity ball in Miami, some 20 years ago, dressed in a blue-sequined dress.

What started as a lark became a habit.

He's not gay, he said.

"I'm not trying to pick up men," he said. "I've got the best-looking girlfriend in town."

The drunken-driving arrest happened on a night when he and his girlfriend, Dorothy, went dancing at Ta-Boo on Worth Avenue.

The police car followed Cargile's Cadillac as he pulled away from the nightspot.

Police, he said, have sometimes been curious when he's out in drag.

"I was walking the dog one night in a dress, and one of them pulled up said, 'Can I have your driver's license?' and I said, 'Does it look like I'm driving?'"

And last year, when he was on his way to Palm Beach Polo and Country Club (where he won a prize in the Easter-bonnet contest), an officer pulled him over just to get a good look at him, he said.

But the night of his drunken-driving arrest was the worst. He's never had trouble like that before.

The officer said Cargile failed a roadside sobriety test and had an open container of alcohol in his car.

"I don't even drink when I go out," Cargile said.

But he blew a 0.14 percent on the breath test — over the legal limit for alcohol.

"I had three glasses of wine for dinner," he said. "Maybe there's something wrong with my system."

But on the night of the arrest, Cargile seemed to have more to say about what's wrong with the legal system.

"Look, back up the damn cops, get them out of this . . . " he said on tape while taking the sobriety tests. "This is a waste of time compared to what is really going on out there."

He told the officers what they really need to do is "to enforce the damn laws."

Which they ended up doing against him.

But not before Cargile let the officers know they were messing with an important man in a red dress.

"I'll never vote for another Democrat," he told the officers. "I told Al Gore that — he is a friend of mine — to straighten your act out."

Which must have sounded even funnier at the time.

"My friends are high-powered state senators," he told the officers.

But it didn't stop the DUI arrest.

Cargile blames John Weiss, the arresting officer.

"He was just one of these kinds of guys," Cargile said. "He's an ex-Marine."

Cargile's public defender is working on his transvestite-discrimination defense, filing a court paper that claims his client "was stopped merely because he chose to wear women's apparel."

Even with the free legal help, Cargile finds it all very aggravating.

"I had to come back from Guyana to go to a hearing," he said.

Cargile's drunken-driving trial was supposed to begin this week in the courtroom of Palm Beach County Judge Susan Lubitz.

But Cargile didn't show up.

"I have malaria," he said. "I have 102-degree fever."

Something he picked up in Guyana, he said.

When Cargile didn't show up, the judge issued a warrant for his arrest. It took Cargile a day and a hospital record to clear that up.

"Can you imagine that?" Cargile said, still apparently miffed at the legal system.

There may be a lesson in this. Although, I doubt Cargile will want to hear it.

I was thinking of something along these lines:

When you get behind the wheel, think twice before you drink and drag.

Palm Beach: "An island off the coast of the United States" 69

Just as we thought:
The sweet smell of success is different in Palm Beach
January 17, 1992

Fruity smells mask seedy core in Palm Beach

Now it's official.

What gets flushed down toilets in Palm Beach really doesn't stink.

I suspected as much. People in the town have always acted that way.

But now, I find out, it's literally true. The town Public Works Department puts perfumed scents in the sewer system every week — vanilla, cherry, citrus. This is lilac week.

All over town, the rich and famous are pushing the lever and sending another bouquet coursing through the dark, fragrant underbelly of this gilded, carefree burg.

Palm Beachers have a fixation with disposal issues. That's why there's daily garbage pickup, no cemeteries and perfumed sewers.

Sure, you can mock them. But I won't. I'm jealous.

I checked with Boca Raton, where I live, and found out that my contributions to the wastewater system get rather rough treatment.

"Fragrances don't help remove the hydrogen sulfide," explained Boca's utilities director, James Chansler, "They just hide it."

"You can either mask or filter odors," he explained. "Boca filters the odors through caustic soda and activated carbon."

Caustic soda. Activated carbon. It sounds so brutal.

Nothing like a vanilla treatment.

The fragrances used in Palm Beach don't do anything to the hydrogen sulfide – the rotten egg smell that breeds in sewers. They just overpower that stink with a more pleasant smell.

"It's like putting on an after-shave without taking a shower," explained Erik Olson, the director of utilities in West Palm Beach.

So in other words, it's a pleasant, sweet facade over a stinking, rotting pustule of foulness. Sounds like a metaphor for Palm Beach itself.

Lake Worth and West Palm Beach do some dabbling in the fragrant sewer trade too, but the people there don't have their hearts into it the way Palm Beach does.

"It's a strange psychology using these things," Olson said. "We've had people complain about the fragrances we used."

So West Palm Beach also uses something called Eliminol, a fragrance that doesn't smell.

Sounds pretty wimpy to me, like playing for a tie. I'm with Palm Beach — go all the way. Make it fruity!

Now, you're probably saying to yourself, "Gee, I was walking in Palm Beach recently, and I didn't notice any cherry aroma drifting up through the sewers."

That's because you really can't smell it.

"If you smell it, it would be by accident," the town's Public Works Director Al Dusey said. "We don't want it wafting about the town."

Unless you go rooting around a pumping station, you wouldn't know what the fragrance of the week is.

Some of you might be saying, "Then why bother?" But you're thinking of this the wrong way. Don't look at it as sanitation. Think of it as conceptual art.

Let me explain.

In 1977, artist Walter DeMaria drilled a 1-kilometer-deep hole into the ground, put a 1-kilometer-long brass rod in the hole, and then covered the hole with a metal plate. It cost $300,000 to do this.

His piece, titled "Vertical Kilometer," was a great work of conceptual art. You couldn't actually see it. But you knew it was there.

It's the same thing with lilac-scented sewer water. Just knowing it's there makes all the difference.

It's not disgusting. It's art.

So for you people on the mainland, the next time you find yourself in the restroom of a Palm Beach restaurant, pull the lever with confidence, knowing that in some small way, you've made the world a little sweeter.

You'll have to imagine that several yards under your feet, there's a liquid garden of lilac, a fragrant memento to Mother Nature from the island of beautiful people.

Palm Beach catfight is all over who gets to a checkout lane first
March 30, 1994

Market brawl proof life doesn't imitate art in Palm Beach

Poor Pat Booth. She has spent years cultivating the image of Palm Beach as an enclave of wealth, style and relentless social posturing. And what happens?

She gets herself into a crotch-kicking, finger-gnawing fight with a pugilistically gifted maid at the Palm Beach Publix.

And over what? Over who gets to a checkout lane first. Poor Pat Booth. So common.

Booth is the author of the novel *Palm Beach*, a steamy tale of sex, power, social climbing, sex, aerobics, money, sex, clothing descriptions and sex.

The book's plot doesn't have much in common with the real-life plot that unfolded when Booth, 51, went *mano a mano* with Muriel Grant, 63, of West Palm Beach.

Unless you count that in both arenas, Booth didn't waste much time before going for the midsection.

Palm Beach patrolman James Dean tried to sort it out in his report, which he wrote in a non-florid style I found refreshing.

"At this time it appears the altercation reference Booth kicking Grant in the pelvic area and Grant hitting Booth's face and biting Booth's finger is not in question," the officer wrote. "However, there is conflicting statements as to who started the altercation."

While the police sort this one out, I think it would be interesting to contrast the glamorous fictional world of Palm Beach with the gritty real-life world of Palm Beach, according to the police report.

The other woman:

In Booth novel: Jo-Anne Duke, the fashion model wife of a "disgustingly rich" oil-money heir.

In Booth real-life drama: Muriel Grant, maid.

Description of the other woman:

In Booth novel: She "was made chiefly of beautifully constructed, if a little underworked, muscle, ligament, tendon and bone. Aerobics had kept her fit, massage had made her sleek and smooth . . ."

In Booth real-life drama: 5-foot-3, 172 pounds.

Mouth action:

In Booth novel: "Occasionally there was the sharp touch of teeth, and the momentary excitement of delicious pain as Lisa fought back for her share of ecstasy, taking the aggressive tongue between the pure white teeth, nipping, nibbling, disciplining it before succumbing once again to its infinitely welcome dictates."

In Booth real-life drama: "According to Ms. Grant, . . . she bit Booth's finger in self-defense saying that Booth was striking her in the face . . . The bite went through the finger bone and Booth has already lost her fingernail on that finger."

Groin action:

In Booth novel: "Like sleepwalkers they moved as one, dancing to an ancient rhythm that had never been taught, never explained."

In Booth real-life drama: "Booth did state that she did kick Grant in the pelvic area . . ."

The dangers of Palm Beach:

In Booth novel: "In Palm Beach the hottest game in town was social climbing. There at least people got hurt. They didn't bleed openly, but they made up for that in the quantity and quality of their tears."

In Booth real-life drama: "Pat Booth and Muriel Grant were in a long checkout line with their carts. At this time a new checkout line next to the one they were in opened up for business. Both parties headed for the open line at the same time."

Travel:

In Booth novel: "He had no time to take in the haunting beauty of the sunlight on the aquamarine sea between Bequia and St. Vincent, still less to pick out and identify the extraordinary houses set like jewels in the rich landscape of the island below."

In Booth real-life drama: "Both parties were taken to Good Samaritan Hospital by Palm Beach Fire/Rescue."

The discomfort of the main character:

In Booth novel: "This should have been paradise - mingling with the mighty in perhaps the prettiest home on the most beautiful island in the world."

In Booth real-life drama: "I had an operation. The whole bone is shattered. I had to be on a drip at the hospital."

A Diamond in the rough in Palm Beach
January 16, 2011

Satire lost on town's defender of the rich

"Do you agree?" Palm Beach Town Councilman Bill Diamond wrote me.

Diamond considers me a kindred soul after the column I wrote last week about his suggestion that Publix give Palm Beachers discount coupons to compensate for the inconvenience of making island residents shop at a West Palm Beach Publix while the town's supermarket undergoes a nine-month renovation.

I suggested that the coupons be on card stock with smudge-free ink, and possibly embossed. Diamond took that as me being in his corner, and wrote that he "deeply appreciated" my column.

"As you rightly point out, this would be more than just a good will gesture but would be of real help to those Palm Beachers who live on limited budgets and who now will be required to spend money on taxi rides to other locations to obtain the necessities of daily life," he wrote.

I figured that I had underestimated Diamond. Judging from that reply, I reassessed him as mature stylist in the art of satire.

So I parried back with my best dose of snark: "You know me, Bill. I'm always looking out for the downtrodden."

And he e-mailed back a remarkably straight-faced reply: "And rightly so, many thanks for helping those who cannot help themselves."

Whoa! That's when it dawned on me that I was dealing with a master humorist.

After all, Diamond was the Palm Beach leader who suggested two years ago that the town secede from the rest of Palm Beach County because the town's wealthy taxpayers were seeing too much of their money go to pay for services for the poorer folks on the other side of the Intracoastal.

Now he was characterizing this same island of privilege and wealth as a haven for the needy.

I began to allow that Diamond might be more than a deft practitioner of the ironic arts: He might be a modern-day Mark Twain.

And yet in the back of my mind I had the opposite thought: that maybe he really did think my embossed-coupon idea was heartfelt.

That's when he sent me that "Do you agree?" e-mail with his latest suggestion in the battle to get Publix to compensate islanders for the inconvenience caused by the remodeling.

Diamond wrote that the supermarket chain should "initiate a shuttle service between the town and one or more of their stores in West Palm Beach on a regular basis so that persons on the Island who can not access those stores because of physical and/or financial reasons will be able to do so."

A freakin' supermarket trolley for Palm Beachers! Scratch Mark Twain.

Diamond had just been elevated to Jonathan Swift status.

At this point, I saw my role as straight man.

"Are there a significant number of poor people in Palm Beach who don't have access to a vehicle, or can't pay for the gas to make a five-mile round trip a couple of times a week?" I wrote.

Diamond responded that there might be "a good number of people" who would use a supermarket shuttle to West Palm Beach.

"Palm Beach is now a year-round community with many people not having summer homes up north to retreat to," he wrote.

I craved a deeper dip into the vat of his caustic wit. So I had to talk to him on the phone, where we could refine his Swiftian idea of a kind of Century Village trolley for Palm Beach.

Would the supermarket trolley in Palm Beach have to ring a bell to pick up riders? And how loud would that bell have to ring to be heard by the needy people hunkering in their oceanfront homes, private clubs or behind their 12-foot hedges?

And that's when I was disappointed. Because after talking with Diamond, I realized that he was dead serious.

"I didn't say we have a lot of poor people," he said. "We just have some."

He said the supermarket shuttle could be a low-key affair. Maybe one or two trips a week done on a schedule made public to island residents.

"We're not talking about a public transportation type of thing," he said.

"It could be a help to people who can't afford a taxi to West Palm

Beach to get the necessities they need."

I waited for the ironic chuckle at the end of that gem. But there was none.

Keeping the common folk from using your Starbucks
October 13, 2006

How to keep Worth Avenue stay brief

To: Starbucks Coffee Co.

From: Cerabino & Associates, Consultants at Large

Subject: Advice on your new Worth Avenue store

First of all, congratulations on your hard-fought victory in getting approval from the town of Palm Beach.

It's no small feat getting the town council to allow something so universally desirable as a coffee shop on Worth Avenue.

In case you haven't figured it out yet, the goal of Palm Beach is to create commerce that would only be desirable and affordable to the people who actually live in town.

And although your coffee is certainly overpriced, it isn't so expensive that it would keep somebody from the other side of the bridge from actually buying a cup.

This is a very big problem for you.

If you don't believe me, walk across the street and talk to the people at the Neiman Marcus. When the town council approved that store in 1998, it tried to get the department store to agree that it wouldn't advertise in any way that might attract nonresidents to shop there.

So, your goal, Starbucks, is to make your coffee shop seem like a private coffee shop, rather than a place that serves the caffeine addiction needs of the greater Palm Beach County community.

And being that you won approval this week by only a 3-2 vote, I think it's important for you to get off on the right foot, to show the people in Palm Beach that you have no intention of serving coffee to anybody but them.

Here are some suggestions that will help you along those lines:

1. The Starbucks sign must go

The recognizable green Starbucks sign would be a magnet for passersby. This is something to avoid. Remember, you must find a way to repel nonresidents from your business. So if you must have a sign over your door, it should say something like "Private Entrance" or "Trespassers will be Violated."

2. Establish a membership fee

Don't think of the Worth Avenue Starbucks as a coffee shop. Think of it as a coffee club, where potential customers pay an initiation fee to become members. Start with something reasonable, say $10,000. That ought to scare away the Palm Tran bus riders.

3. Initiate a guest rule

Hey, it worked for the Everglades Club. The gist is that members aren't allowed in the store with guests who themselves wouldn't be suitable as members. This would keep domestic help from walking in with their employers.

4. Pick up your employees at the bridge

You can't run a coffee shop without hiring people for modest wages. This is a tremendous problem for you. Some of these employees will have disreputable-looking cars, which they will park on Palm Beach. Not acceptable.

The solution is that they all park in West Palm Beach and walk across the middle bridge, where you will pick them up for work, then drop them off at the end of the day. It's the least you can do.

5. Improve the uniform

The standard Starbucks garb won't cut it here. Lose the green aprons. Then walk down the street and buy a bunch of Hermes scarves. That will get you started in the right direction.

6. Nobody uses the restrooms

And we mean nobody. The Starbucks restrooms, while required by law, should be for decorative purposes only, remaining off-limits to employees and customers. The town went through a lot of trouble to have a public beach without public restrooms. You don't want to destroy that by having a coffee shop within walking distance to the beach that might provide a little relief.

7. Go out of business quickly

It won't be hard if you follow the first six suggestions.

**Keeping up with the Figg-Tagles,
or how to get into Social Index-Directory**
January 16, 1994

Social directory closes the book on Vista del Vern

The new Social Index-Directory is out in Palm Beach, and the chances are excellent that you're not in it.

I know I'm not. I checked. If I were in it, I would have been there between the Cayzers (Major Harold and his lovely wife, Beatrice de Holguin Fairbanks) and the Chalks (Roy O. and Claire, and their lovely 100-foot sailboat, Blue Horizon Le Quatre).

I'm not surprised. After all, I don't even have a Blue Horizon Le One yet.

And as I read the fine print, I could see that my could-have-been page mates — the Cayzers and the Chalks — were leaving me in the dust in the all-important "clubs" category.

Between them, they belong to . . .

Bath and Tennis, Old Guard, Buck's, Cavalry and Guards, King's, Royal Channel Islands Yacht, White's (London), Collete, Palm Beach Country, Governors, Palm Beach Yacht, Friars, Le Club, Marco Polo (N.Y.), Woodmont Country (D.C.), Newport Yacht (R.I.), Yacht Club de Monaco, and the Ladies Annexe Boodle's.

I belong to ... Come to think of it, I don't belong to any club. I used to be in a book-of-the-month club, but I got tired of getting ones I didn't want to read.

And as for those other clubs, well, I have no idea how a lady annexes her boodle.

Or for that matter, how a person gets included in the Social Index-Directory. So I called the publisher, Susan Devoy.

"How did you get a copy?" she asked, alarmed.

(Now I know how Julia Roberts felt in *The Pelican Brief*.)

"Well, I was just wondering what it takes to get in the book, that's all," I said.

No sense mentioning how light my social calendar is. I would have to play to my strengths.

But after perusing the directory, I realized I didn't have many picture cards in my deck.

A good way to get in the book, it seems, is to have a department store named after you. There's Mrs. J.C. Penney in there, and a Woolworth woman.

Another good way is to marry someone with a great hyphenated name, like Polly Figg-Tagle.

She's in the book. If only my wife had a name like Polly Figg-Tagle, I'd be set.

The social directory also lists "other addresses," which is another potential problem, considering I have only one. And my home doesn't have a name.

That's the other thing. People in the social directory name their homes.

The Leddys call their Maine home Camp Tam-Tom. The Buswells' summer home is called Stillington Hall. The Teasdales live in Quack Hollow, the Scaravillis at Playwood. And the Wyckoff Myers have dubbed their New York home Puddingstone.

Sounds more like a urinary tract problem.

I can call my place Vista del Vern.

Spanish is very big for home nicknames. There are a bunch of Casa de something-or-others. Nearly anything sounds elegant in Spanish or Italian.

Some guy in the directory named his house Casa Bianca Al Lago. Which is a fancy way of saying he's got a white house facing the Intracoastal.

So Vista del Vern is a fancy way of saying that I have a view of my next-door-neighbor, Vern.

The "yacht" entry will definitely be a problem, and I'm not sure whether "Delta frequent flyer card" is an acceptable entry for "airplane."

"Suppose I fake it," I tell the the directory publisher. "Suppose I just give you a name of a yacht. Would you check it?"

"Yes," Devoy said. "Some guy once said he went to an out-of-the-way military school and claimed he was a baron. We checked."

"So how can I . . ."

"I don't think you'll be in it," she said.

She explained the nomination process, and the review board.

She's right. I won't be in it.

"But you let Rose Kennedy in," I said, in a final bit of protest. "How social can she be, she's barely alive?"

"We get the card back every year on her," Devoy answered, "so we keep putting her in."

The annual directory began in 1923 as an unofficial Palm Beach phone book, a way for the swells to know who to call at party time.

"This has been a tough year for the directory," Devoy said. "We had a lot of people die this year."

But others have filled the ranks, she said.

The good life continues at Puddingstone, at the Ladies Annexe Boodle's Club, and wherever else Figg-Tagles meet.

"We don't want any publicity," Devoy said.

I could see her point.

Weekend at Bernie's – Madoff -style
March 18, 2009

Make Madoffs' home time-share for fraud victims

Bernie Madoff's wife needs to give up her Palm Beach home.

Ruth Madoff got a homestead exemption on her waterfront Lake Trail home while her husband's grand swindle was about to unravel, and her lawyers will certainly make the dubious case that poor Mrs. M. was an unwitting bystander to her husband's fraud. But whether or not she's legally entitled to shield the multimillion-dollar Florida home under state law is beside the point.

How could she ever want to live in Palm Beach, to face so many of the people who were ripped off by her husband?

She'd be a pariah on the level of a Holocaust denier.

The only decent thing for Ruth Madoff to do is to hand over the keys and disappear into the deep, dark night.

And beside, I've got a plan for the home.

The Madoff swindle is a financial crime so deep that its victims need a time – and place – of mourning and consolation. Just as many people needed to come to ground zero in New York after the terrorist attacks of 9/11 as a way to grieve or feel a sense of solidarity with the victims, Madoff's chicanery deserves a gathering site.

Why not the couple's Palm Beach home?

Federal prosecutors have already announced they're planning to seize the Palm Beach home, along with the Madoffs' Manhattan penthouse and French country home, both also listed only under Ruth Madoff's name. The feds will try to get everything: the yacht, the fishing boat, the cars, the Steinway piano, the home furnishings, the silverware, the cash, the bank accounts and whatever else turns up.

All the couple's assets will be sold off, and victims of the scheme will get some payment.

But these partial repayments won't make the victims whole again. Not in any real sense.

They need something more.

And this is where my plan comes in. Instead of seizing and selling the Palm Beach home, the home should be maintained as a time-share available to all of Madoff's victims and their heirs.

They would all be entitled to time based on the amount of money they lost.

Victims would be free to transfer their time-share days to other victims, helping to build a network of support and commiseration among them.

I know what you're thinking: "Frank, why would victims of Bernie Madoff's scheme ever want to stay in his home?"

For one reason, every room would be outfitted with a video screen that is directly linked to a video feed from Madoff's prison cell. So that while you're lounging in his former home, and sitting on the expensive furniture he bought with your retirement money, you can look up any time you want and see him in his Spartan prison cell.

As the Sicilians say, revenge is a dish that must be eaten cold – and this one's got frost on it.

There you are, looking at sunset over the Intracoastal, a glass of fine wine in your hand, and you can look up at Bernie Madoff staring at a cinder block wall, and perhaps, it will lead to whatever comes

Palm Beach: "An island off the coast of the United States"

after anger in the grieving process.

By keeping the Palm Beach home, rather than cashing it out as just another asset, the place will also double as a function site for all the charities defrauded by Madoff as well as a kind of national monument to the nation's biggest Ponzi scheme.

It will be the place where the Madoff crimes will be marked, and where its victims can come to lay wreaths to properly mourn their dearly departed nest eggs.

And it will be the only Madoff investment that will actually grow in value over time.

As for his wife, Ruth Madoff should develop a sense of shame, call off her lawyers and consider herself lucky if she manages to hightail it out of Palm Beach with all her jewelry.

CHAPTER 7
News from the strip club
Somebody's got to do it

A shocking new device at T's Lounge
January 08, 2003

Here's another shocking exposé on strip clubs

I walk into T's Lounge.

It's the middle of the afternoon, not exactly prime time in the strip club business. Nobody is stirring at The Wheel of Friction game. The lone dancer on stage is in power-save mode, and the guys at the bar are distracted by their own conversation. The mood in the darkened room seems more sleepy than sultry. But not for me. No, I'm pretty hopped-up.

You see, I'm here to see something new.

This is, after all, T's Lounge, a Palm Beach County institution that brought creamed-corn wrestling to South Florida, a sport that was canned even before it was canned.

And once again, T's appears to be leading the way with a shocking new innovation in the local strip club scene.

So I wait patiently at the bar, until one of the managers motions me to follow him. We walk through the lounge, and stop at a door with a combination lock.

He punches in the numbers, opens the door, and takes me upstairs, past the dancers' undressing rooms and into an office of sorts above the stage.

General manager Dan O'Connell is sitting there at his desk. He's behind a computer screen, doing who knows what? Spread sheets, maybe.

"I saw your ad," I say, pulling out a copy of the newspaper advertisement.

"You wanna see it?" he asks.

He brings out a big white cabinet, and removes something that looks like a red flotation device.

"It's idiot-proof," he says. "The machine knows what to do."

He presses a button on the device's exterior, and a mechanical voice fills the room.

"Apply pads to person's bare chest," the machine commands.

(That shouldn't be tough to do around here.)

Then he shows me the paddles. Of the defibrillator.

You know you're in South Florida when a strip club has heart-resuscitation equipment, which it advertises as "New!" — as if a defibrillator ranks right up there with the Kitty Kat Karousel and the Wheel of Friction as a reason to go.

T's Lounge got the machine a couple of weeks ago, and trained eight members of its staff in a four-hour course, O'Connell says. The device, which uses paddles to shock someone in cardiac arrest, will be mounted by the bar, he says.

Theoretically, it will spare the lives of men who might otherwise die of embarrassment if they died in a strip club.

O'Connell says the club bought the machine, thinking it would make an interesting marketing tool, as well as a safety feature, even though he can't remember any patron actually having a heart attack in the club.

"But you get sued if you don't do something," he says. "So you might as well do something."

The machine is good for 300 shocks, he says.

"Not that we'll need it for that many."

Which made me wonder . . .

"This isn't something that will be incorporated into any of the dances, will it?" I ask.

"No," O'Connell says. "It's strictly a medical thing."

Oh, well. I thought that maybe the suburban West Palm Beach club would pioneer a new form of entertainment, an amped-up permutation of the lap dance. The zap dance.

"It's going to be locked with an alarm system," O'Connell says.

OK, OK. Strictly medical. OK, I understand.

(Does creamed corn conduct electricity?)

Lap dance hell: Can there be such a thing?
May 16, 1997

Large stripper meets plaintiff in 'Crashdance'

So, Don Allain was just sitting there minding his own business. At least, that's what the 36-year-old Boca Raton man says.

And I believe him. Because that's what most guys do in strip joints — they just sit there minding their own business.

Allain was minding his own business in Tiffany's Cabaret, in Boynton Beach. Sitting there with three of his chums. It was almost midnight.

And then it happened, the event that led to the lawsuit.

I guess you could call it a crass-action lawsuit, a squish-and-fall, or a matter of jurisimprudence.

"One of the dancers walked by," Allain said, "and said, 'Hey, don't look so gloomy.'"

"Then she said I looked cute."

Which under most circumstances is a compliment. But when guys get called "cute" in a strip club, it's kind of like being called "hip" at a Barry Manilow concert or "sensible" at a Star Trek convention.

"The next thing I know, she just sat down on top of me," Allain said.

Or as Allain's personal injury lawyer, Phil Berman, put it: "She insinuated herself on him."

The insinuation of the stripper took the form of a sidesaddle lap-plopping maneuver, with both her arms on his shoulders, Allain said.

Things like this never happen to people who mind their own business in places such as public libraries. And actually, it shouldn't happen at Tiffany's, which has a code of conduct posted near the front door.

Rule No. 2: "No friction/lap dancing"

Rule No. 3: "No foundling by customer or dancer."

Foundling? That sounds like a metallurgical process done on steel to make it stiffer.

"That should be 'fondling,'" explained Tiffany's manager, John Tobin.

News from the strip club: Somebody's got to do it

Oh, I see. Goes to show you. Everybody's minding their business so much, that nobody corrected the spelling error. (Further proof that strip clubs are more concerned with sin tax, than syntax.)

Anyway, back to poor Mr. Allain, who, when we left him, had a stripper insinuated on his lap.

Did I mention she weighed 160 pounds?

I didn't think so. And that's not counting the couple of ounces for the transparent negligee.

At least, that's how much Allain says the woman weighed.

"She was big, about 6 feet tall," he said.

Allain said he weighed about 150 pounds.

"I weighed less than I do now, because then I was still able to do karate and play flag football," he said.

The chair Allain says he was sitting in was one of those bouncy ones that have a sideways "U" shaped metal-bar frame on the base. The open end of the sideways "U" is in the back of the seat.

"She was on me for only a couple seconds, if that, and then the chair broke, folding like an accordion," Allain said.

He went flopping back, with the stripper going for the ride by hanging on to his shoulders with both hands as she fell on top of him, pounding him into the floor.

"She thought it was hilarious," Allain said.

But he didn't. He ended up with a rotator cuff injury and two herniated discs in his lower back, his lawyer said.

Allain, a self-employed cleaning company owner, said he has missed work and can't pick up his three children anymore.

Tobin, the club's manager, said the dancer in question no longer works there, and the club has since gotten new chairs. But not because of Allain's tumble.

Allain's lawyer sued Tiffany's this week in Palm Beach County Circuit Court, claiming that the strip club shouldn't encourage or allow its dancers to sit "on top of the business invitee."

Which I think is going to disappoint a lot of other guys who come there to mind their own business.

The 'bottom' line: God is really for everybody
December 10, 1993

Infant in swaddling clothes tops topless

"I've decided that I want people to remember what Christmas is all about," Joanne McClure says.

She's explaining why she put a nativity scene on the roof of her Boynton Beach business this year. The three plastic figures of Baby Jesus, Mary and Joseph are hooked up for night illumination and adorned with a bunch of hay tossed around the manger. A familiar holiday scene. Except for the other lighted display in front of McClure's business.

The one that says "Topless Go-Go Girls."

Oh, holey nightie!

McClure is explaining the true meaning of Christmas to me as I stand in the dancers' dressing (undressing?) room. It's the only place in Morey's Lounge where you can have a telephone conversation that won't be drowned out by the thumping music.

Kevin, the disc jockey, directed me to the phone there and the lounge owner's voice on the other end of it.

First, I have to wait for the on-deck dancer to finish getting into her costume.

She wears white. Her name is Angel. Hark.

Ye faithful had come to watch, sitting on bar stools in front of a stage adorned with two ceiling-to-floor brass poles that serve as dramatic props.

If you had X-ray eyes, you could see right from the fleshy stage gymnastics to the plastic figures above, where Mary clutches both hands modestly over her plastic chest.

"I'm a born-again Christian," McClure is explaining. "We're not allowed to have nativity scenes in public parks anymore, so I'm having mine on private property."

A born-again topless bar owner sending a message to the community. Further proof that we live in a wonderful world.

Maybe what I had seen on stage was nothing more than a metaphorical interpretation of the separation of church and state.

"Joanne, I imagine that there are people who will see some

contradiction in a nativity display at a topless bar," I say.

"How?" she says. "Christ in his time was a low life. He led Mary Magdalene to the Lord. Paul spent most of his time in jail. Jesus didn't dwell with the Pharisees."

He didn't leer at creamed corn wrestling, either.

I'm no Biblical interpreter. But somehow I had the feeling that McClure had taken this turn-the-other-cheek business the wrong way.

However, theological gyrations aren't my turf. So I let McClure talk.

"The dancers aren't prostituting themselves," she says. "We want everybody to go to church. The people who come here are glad to see the display. A lot of people forget what Christmas is about."

Another dancer walks into the dressing room and gets ready for her show. I forget what Christmas is about.

As for commandments, there's only one on display. It's taped to a mirrored wall. It has a drawing of a nude woman, a hand, and the words:

"Sorry, No Touching."

A message for all seasons.

I'm ill-equipped to get into a religious debate with McClure. I've only been born once.

So I'm going to leave the moralizing up to the professionals. I leave Morey's and make some calls.

"I've seen it," Rev. John Wiley of the First Baptist Church of Boynton Beach says of the nativity display.

"We generally believe that when Jesus has an encounter with people, they turn away from this type of lifestyle.

"I think the purpose of topless dancing is to whet the sexual appetite," Wiley says. "There's nothing sinful in sexual desires. It's what we do with them. These dancers try to put things in people's minds that aren't necessarily what God intended."

The Rev. Dick Laverdure of the Lakeside Christian Center in Boynton Beach said the nativity scene sends the wrong message.

"The scripture says to refrain from the appearances of evil. To me, it would be bringing the Baby Jesus into a very . . . I don't know what the proper wording is . . . a worldly situation," he says. "It's as if he would approve of a topless bar, as if he would sanction that."

Brother Joe Ranieri, who runs a nearby family shelter, says it's just odd.

"Is it better if they had nothing there? I don't know," he says. "I guess God is really for everybody, that's the bottom line."

So maybe it's a decent Christmas message after all, the kind you can only find in a place as unlikely as the top of a topless bar.

Frankly, we don't want to see Rusty and his stripper pole
June 06, 2001

Rusty Libido: Have license, will not strip

I officially entered the ranks of Palm Beach County's licensed strippers this week.

The whole process at the county's office of public safety took less than 15 minutes. It was very unceremonious. There was no written test. I didn't have to demonstrate the equivalent of parallel parking on a sliding pole. And I didn't have to dip anything in a vat of oil while reciting a credo in Latin.

"That's it?" I asked Midge, the county registrar of strippers, after getting my Palm Beach County adult entertainer ID card.

"That's it," she said.

The idea to become a licensed adult entertainer grew out of a recent court decision that held the county is within its rights to require strippers to carry photo-ID county licenses. The county began this program two years ago as a way to keep underage teenage girls from performing in clubs.

A local dancer sued, claiming the registration violated her rights to privacy. A Palm Beach County circuit judge agreed, but an appeals court last month said the county could start licensing strippers again.

And now that the county is "tooled up," as Midge likes to put it, the dancers have been bouncing in for their ID cards at a good clip. (I just missed seeing Sapphire.)

My name was entered into the database joining the ranks of my colleagues: Starburst, Sky, Diamond, Juicy, a bunch of women named

News from the strip club: Somebody's got to do it

after meteorological conditions, and somebody who calls herself Tina the Fire Lady.

I wrote down Rusty Libido as my stage name. But I don't think I'll be doing much dancing.

"I just wanted to get the ID card," I explained to my mother, who was appalled when I told her about my new license.

"That's something that could come back to haunt you," she said. "People could look it up, and it would show you as a stripper."

How bad could it be? It's not like I've been marinating in alcohol most of my life, then decided to run for president.

"I can explain it if anybody asks," I said.

"Just don't tell anybody," she said.

It's too late. In fact, I've already gotten a job offer.

A woman sent me an e-mail offering to hire Rusty Libido for a friend's 80th birthday party.

"I realize you lack experience," she wrote, "but for the right price, this could be your opportunity for a big time."

I had to decline. A big time for me is a movie from Blockbusters and a quart of ice cream.

"Rusty Libido," I explained to my would-be employer, "doesn't have the kind of insurance that allows him to perform for 80-year-olds."

I'm more of a toxic, than exotic dancer. I don't even dance much at weddings, except for those compulsory conga line scenes.

And the only time anybody ever wanted me to strip in a commercial situation involved the words, "Turn your head and cough."

But I'm licensed, that's the important thing.

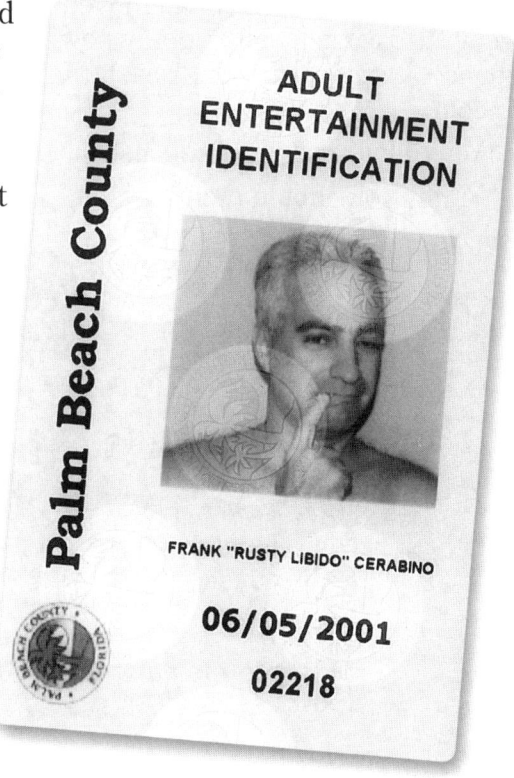

And not only that, but I've determined by perusing the public records of my colleagues that I am the heaviest licensed stripper in Palm Beach County, although at 175 pounds, the dancer who goes by the name "Pebbles" is only a double cheeseburger or two away from claiming the title.

(Pebbles, my eye!)

It wasn't long before I had moved my driver license back one sleeve in my wallet and put my new license in the front slot. And, by chance, I was in the Palm Beach Mall when a reader came up to me to chat.

"You didn't really become a stripper, did you?" she asked.

"Funny you should mention that," I said, pulling out my wallet.

CHAPTER 8
Natural disasters
The hurricanes of 2004 and 2005

Music to his ears: HE'S GOT THE POWER
September 15, 2004

Power is key to reclaiming paradise lost

It was anticlimactic.

After eight days without power, the lights came on in my house, and I wasn't even there. "You have power," my neighbor said, calling me on my cellphone.

For more than a week, it was miserable being in my home, and then, suddenly, I wasn't there when I wanted to be there the most. I had envisioned the moment many times, the lights suddenly popping on, the way they were at 2:45 p.m. on Sept. 4.

Like childbirth, I wanted to be there to witness the magical delivery. I wanted to race for the thermostat on the air conditioner, to turn on all the lights, and to run a victory lap around the storm-shuttered windows.

I wanted to be standing on my swale, waving palm fronds to salute a passing parade of FPL trucks as they drove down the block, liberating us from the netherworld of the powerless, into the world of light, and humidity-scoured coolness.

I wanted to jump in the snow drift of dirty laundry that had gathered by the washing machine. I wanted to stand on my roof and scream, "I HAVE POWER!"

I couldn't wait to rush home and do it all. Turn on the TV. Toss something frozen in the microwave. Put my ear up to the reassuring hum of the refrigerator — that is, once it was rid of the swamp-like gases wafting out of its opened doors.

I wanted to turn the pool pump on, set the clocks to the proper time, and stow all the flashlights out of sight again.

I wanted to quickly get the idea that South Florida, my home for the past 20 years, might actually once again return to a place worthy of habitation.

Because for the past week, I had begun to wonder, to marvel, even, at the completely artificial arrangement we've struck with nature in this part of the world. Without the modern convenience of electricity, we're quickly reduced to a nomadic tribe of grumpy misfits looking for free ice.

It's remarkable that an area so blithely referred to as "paradise" can turn into hell so quickly, and thoroughly.

It felt defeating, not to be able to feel comfortable in your own home. To have to be out in the world, at restaurants, at friends' houses, at a mall — someplace other than your own little sanctuary, that dark, sticky place that had changed from a home into a huge, unwelcoming storage shed for your things.

I could think of nothing more appealing than feeling normal again. To eat at home. To fall asleep watching TV. To get up in the morning and make a pot of coffee, rather than getting in line at the Dunkin' Donuts.

To have the luxury of feeling bored by routine, even.

Within a few hours, the hurricane shutters were down and put away. Kids were swimming in the pool, and the house felt cool again.

Lights were on everywhere. Music was coming from the CD player. The washing machine was churning. Desktop computer monitors were aglow.

The empty, clean refrigerator was begging for a fresh start.

Sunlight poured in the house, but it wasn't the malicious sunshine that came through open windows, overwhelming the inside of the house with heat and humidity. It was sunshine on a leash, sealed off from the house by closed windows, and by central air conditioning that more than neutralized its heat.

It was paradise again. Or at least, that artificial brand of paradise we've carved out for ourselves here in this tropical swampland that used to be largely uninhabited for a very good reason.

No more Kumbaya: After the storm camaraderie is ending
October 27, 2005

Post-Wilma honeymoon won't last much longer

The camp-out phase is quickly coming to an end.

I'm still clinging to it tenaciously, giving it my best isn't-it-great-to-meet-the-neighbors spirit! The morning after the storm, I wandered my neighborhood with an empty coffee cup. I didn't have far to go before I smelled a pot brewing on a camping stove inside a neighbor's garage. Within a few minutes, there was a crowd of us huddling around the pot, and making our awkward, much-belated introductions.

"I just met the people behind us," explained one woman, "and we've been neighbors for seven years."

Then she looked at me and said, "You're . . . you're the guy that walks the little dog."

That's how it is in those first couple of days. Lots of neighborhood camaraderie, as we share power tools, pass along scouting reports from the Home Depot, and enjoy a moveable feast at backyard gas grills with their smoke signals of invitation.

At first, it's a wondrous new world of pot-luck dinners, rediscovered board games, and the joys of the simple life. No work. No school. No TV. No Internet. No laundry. No schedule. No problem.

Life unplugged. We've taken a leap back a hundred years,

synchronizing our activities with the sun, making do with less, and finding something charming in it all.

"And how about that night sky!" I say. "We need to take advantage of this."

I lay in my backyard hammock, listening to music on my iPod, with the noise-canceling headphones blocking out the sound of my neighbor's generator. I hadn't seen a sky like this since my Navy days. And then, on cue, a shooting star whizzed by to the accompaniment of James Taylor.

This isn't so bad, I think.

But what I've learned last year from Hurricane Frances was that this initial camp-out phase is a fragile thing, a fleeting honeymoon of optimism that yields to something gloomy, and ultimately, angry.

The first phase of post-hurricane survival lasts only two or three days. A leading indicator of its demise is when it first occurs to you that eating an Oreo cookie no longer sounds like a treat.

When that happens, look out. You're headed for a mood swing. What also happens by then is that you start hearing word about power being restored elsewhere.

"I hate you," I heard my daughter jokingly telling one of her friends on the phone.

She was reacting to the news that in Palm Beach Gardens, not only is the power on in many areas, but The Gardens mall is open for business.

A key component in the camp-out phase is the feeling that we're all in this together. When you start seeing lights on the horizon and you encounter people who appear to be enjoying daily hot showers, the romance you once had with the simple life quickly starts to wane.

By then, your laundry has hit a crisis level, the frozen meat you ate during those first few days is gone, and the neighborhood has split into the generator haves and the generator have-nots.

The next thing you know, you start hanging out in public places with power, just to be in the air conditioning, just to reconnect with your old life.

You start fantasizing about squandering ice, and checking your e-mail, and being somewhere other than your dark house. And those stars in the sky, they don't look as bright anymore.

I can see this next phase creeping up on me, but I'm going to hold it off as much as possible. I'm going to try to think positive, and tell myself that the glass is half-full — and not try to think too hard about the liquid in that glass, and whether it needs to be boiled.

Intersection etiquette after hurricanes, and those who ignore it
October 30, 2005

6 'dark' personalities drive us crazy at intersections

I never thought I'd be writing something nice about traffic lights.

But here goes. I'm looking forward to driving up to a red light again. Navigating through busy intersections without traffic lights has its cowboy charm, but as the days go by, I find myself marking my roadway journeys by how many precarious unmarked intersections I still have to cross.

Intersections such as Military Trail and Okeechobee Boulevard or Glades Road and U.S. 441 are dangerous enough with traffic lights. Without them, they're a rolling game of chicken.

Part of the problem may be that we, as a community, are not well-suited to group behavior that requires uniform displays of patience and courtesy.

These unregulated intersections work only if each car stops, and if the one that has stopped the longest goes first. But that's not always what happens.

And here's why. I've identified the six basic driver profiles that make these intersections more dramatic than they need to be:

Mr. Electricity

This is the driver who believes that, as long as he is within a few inches of the car in front of him, he is connected to that car. And that car's full stop counts for him, too.

This concept of electricity is borrowed from the childhood game of hide-and-seek, when captured prisoners hold hands as a way to be freed as a group when only one person is touched. It is, however, not a concept always recognized by the three other drivers at an intersection.

Natural disasters: The hurricanes of 2004 and 2005

And, yes, Mr. Electricity is certainly a guy.

The Orchestra Conductor

This is the driver who appears to be directing a symphony at the intersection.

The rules of the road are pretty simple here and do not require arm waving.

And yet, this Seiji Osawa of Okeechobee Boulevard feels the need to direct a series of hand signals to the other drivers.

What usually complicates the situation is that The Orchestra Conductor decides who should be going in an order that has nothing to do with who arrived first at that intersection.

The Midwesterner

It's never his turn. This is a driver who is too polite for his own good.

If you don't go when it is your turn, you're not being nice; you're being a hazard to navigation. The whole intersection comes to a perplexing halt by your "consideration."

Everyone waits for you to go, and then when you don't, they all go. Usually at the same time.

The Premature Accelerator

This is the driver who jumps out too soon, then loses his nerve somewhere near the middle of the intersection. He stops, then takes another look around to reassess his options. This causes a condition known as Trafficus Interruptus, paralyzing other drivers who are now unwilling to move an inch until The Premature Accelerator is back in motion and well out of collision range.

The New Yorker

What other cars?

The Big Dog

This is the driver who knows he's in the right-of-weight-mobile. The jumbo SUV. The 18-wheeler. The pickup hauling a trailer.

When this guy pulls up to the intersection, he does a brief, dismissive survey of the other puny excuses of gas-burning platforms, turning otherwise sensible drivers into The

Midwesterner. That is, except for the guy behind The Big Dog, who thinks this is a good time to become Mr. Electricity.

The Big Dog plows ahead, expecting fully that the guy across the street in the Daewoo is going to acknowledge the right of weight. Little does he know, though, that the guy in the Daewoo may be The New Yorker.

CHAPTER 9
Man-made disasters
Trump and Limbaugh

Donald Trump's flagpole at Mar-a-Lago ruffles feathers in Palm Beach
Nov. 1, 2006

Long and short of it: It's all about the pole

Everybody's got this Donald Trump flag story all wrong.

It's not about the flag. It's about the pole.

And what's amazing is that Trump settled for such a small flagpole.

Let me back up and explain.

Without getting zoning approval, Trump put an 80-foot flagpole in the front yard of the Mar-a-Lago Club in Palm Beach. He immediately began flying a jumbo American flag on the rogue flagpole — not the first schemer to cover his tracks with a patriotic feint.

But the real issue here is the flagpole. It has the unfortunate distinction of being both too big for the town and not big enough for Trump.

First, let's look at it from the town's perspective: The flagpole is an affront to the town's rigorously defended zoning code, which has set

Man-made disasters: Trump and Limbaugh

a 42-foot pole limit.

And with Trump, you've got to figure that the American flag that's up there now is just a place-holder to leverage approval for the pole. Once the pole is unchallenged, he can fly something more suitable to his tastes - a red, yellow and black banner with the word "Trump" in letters big enough to be seen across the Intracoastal.

So the town, in an effort to avoid being branded as unpatriotic, will have to focus its complaints on the pole, while Trump pretends it's all about his unquenchable patriotic yearnings.

But the pole is really Trump's prize, too.

Let's look at things from his perspective: The real estate market is tanking. The shine is off his TV show, *The Apprentice*. And his newlywed days are over. He's just another frumpy, ever-expanding middle-age husband somewhere on life's back nine.

This is midlife crisis time. Time to get yourself a big pole.

But that's my main beef with Trump here. His pole just isn't big enough, certainly not up to Trump standards of excess.

Sure, he can say he's got the biggest pole in Palm Beach, but that's like saying you've got the biggest tofu concession at a NASCAR track.

I talked with Mark Peterson, who owns H.A. Peterson & Sons, a flagpole supplier in Miami. I asked him about Trump's 80-foot pole, and how impressive that was in the pantheon of poledom.

"There are tons of 80-foot poles out there," Peterson said. "That's like the ones you see at the car dealers."

So unless his secret plan is to turn the club into Mar-a-Lago Motors, it looks like, for once, Donald Trump ... oh, I can't believe I'm going to say this ... came up short while making a public display of his ego.

If you want to see a big pole, you've got to see the one that Peterson erected for boxing promoter Don King, outside King's offices in Deerfield Beach. You can see that one from I-95, near the Hillsboro Boulevard exit.

Don King's flagpole is a 150-foot spire of steel, and it's flanked by a pair of 100-foot flagpoles.

Trump would have to double the size of his pole to have a bigger one than King.

So, I feel a little bad for Trump. Bad that he has gotten so far off his game. Bad that he didn't try to get a bigger pole than the 150-footer that King has lurking just over the horizon.

So, here's my suggestion. The town ought to just consider itself lucky and turn a blind eye to Trump's pole.

A younger Trump would have ordered up a 151-foot pole. Antagonizing him now over such a mediocre attempt at excess might be considered cruel, and possibly costly in litigation.

He's at a fragile stage of life. The smart thing to do might just be to present him with a bronze plaque of thanks and inscribe it: "To Donald Trump, in appreciation for his enormous flagpole, the biggest pole on Palm Beach."

It's the least we could do to help him through this crisis.

Limbaugh's leanings are to the wrong side in Palm Beach County
Sept. 14, 2007

Rush needs some exit ideas for this quagmire

Rush Limbaugh needs to leave Palm Beach County.

He is very uncomfortable around us. "They are deranged," he said on his radio show this week, claiming that an alarming number of Palm Beach County residents are "devoid of any rationality or reason."

Apparently, this is because we're high on something.

"They've drunk the Kool-Aid down here, folks, and they drink it every day," Limbaugh told his audience.

I know what you're thinking: Wasn't Limbaugh the guy who got busted for the drugs?

Hate to quibble, but it's not like we're the ones who had to cop a plea on a drug charge and whiz into a cup for 18 months.

Even so, we're apparently so horrible that it has made Limbaugh a virtual prisoner in his oceanfront Palm Beach home.

"It's one of the reasons I don't cross the bridge here much," Limbaugh told his radio audience, "except ... to like go to the airport and get out."

Man-made disasters: Trump and Limbaugh

You see? Limbaugh wants to get out.

It might not be such a bad idea.

Sometimes, when you go into a place where you don't belong and encounter a hostile population that doesn't share your world view, the best thing to do is get out.

Limbaugh's foolhardy occupation of a liberal part of Florida was probably a mistake right from the start. Bad intelligence.

He thought he possessed weapons of mass persuasion, but it turned out to be just a lot of nonsense. He thought we'd greet him as an intellectual liberator, without a clue as to how repulsive he'd turn out to be.

And so now he is scrambling for a rosy interpretation of a tough set of facts. That must be why he thinks it's our fault that we don't agree with his political views.

"If you want to know how kooky they are, you ought to pick up any South Florida newspaper," he told his audience.

Limbaugh vented about us as a way to disparage Rep. Robert Wexler, D-Delray Beach, who had questioned Gen. David Petraeus about the wisdom of keeping American forces in Iraq.

"The American people are skeptical," Wexler told Petraeus, "because four years ago very credible people, both in uniform and not in uniform, came before this Congress and sold us a bill of goods that turned out to be false."

Limbaugh said Wexler was just saying that to placate us kooks.

"He knows how wacko they are, and he's gotta represent them," Limbaugh said.

Hate to quibble, again. But the American people were actually sold a bill of goods on Iraq four years ago. Although in Limbaugh's defense, he might have missed it. The Iraq-as-bogeyman charade was presented around the time Limbaugh was zonked out on OxyContin.

The important thing here is for us to stop fighting and start being reasonable.

Limbaugh needs to pull out, and we'd love to get rid of him.

We just need to figure out a workable exit strategy.

The problem will be to overcome Limbaugh's fixation for declaring "victory." It's a ridiculous word to use in the context of Iraq.

But Limbaugh, who is childless and missed his own chance to fight for his country due to a convenient cyst on his El Rushbo, is heartily in favor of sending other people's children to die for "victory."

At this point, "victory" has been downsized to mean running out the clock on this administration so that the architects and cheerleaders of this war won't be held accountable for the inevitable pullout.

So here's my suggestion:

Let's give Limbaugh his "victory" in Palm Beach County.

The easiest way to get rid of him may be as simple as hanging a few banners on the bridges to Palm Beach. They'd say:

"Mission Accomplished, Rush."

Trump's full page ad doesn't 'own up' to the facts
Nov. 26, 1993

Baby blues blur
The Donald's view of reality

Postpartum depression happens to some people.

Those first few weeks after childbirth can be a bummer. Hormone imbalances, a lack of confidence, and the crushing and often anticlimactic responsibility of parenting sometimes close in. Supposedly this only happens to women.

But I think Donald Trump's got it.

That's the only explanation that makes sense.

The Trumpster must have a low-down, mind-messin' case of the postpartum blues.

What other excuse could there be for the full-page ad he took in *The Palm Beach Daily News*.

"Success Story: 1990s" it read at the top.

Most of the page was dominated by a picture of Trump Plaza, the twin-tower, 33-story condo building on Flagler Drive in West Palm Beach.

And under the picture, a block of text explained:

"This is an advertisement taken to explain the great success of a development, Trump Plaza of the Palm Beaches, of which many people, until recently, had not been fully aware."

It carries on in his subtle self-congratulatory way for another eight sentences before this rousing finale:

"When I look at Trump Plaza from Mar-a-Lago, I am proud that even in the horrendous real estate market of the early 1990s, I was able to rescue this previously troubled and unsold development, add management, construction expertise and the name Trump . . . and make it into one of Florida's great success stories."

It's a stunning ad.

Mainly because he doesn't even own Trump Plaza any more.

A bunch of banks took it away from him two years ago because he couldn't repay the loans he took to buy it. This newspaper carried a stack of stories about it.

Which raises the question:

Why is he now taking a full-page advertisement to brag about something he doesn't own anymore? Something he lost. Something he was lucky to weasel out of without having to pay the $14 million loan guarantee he signed for when he bought it.

The answer, I'm afraid, is simple.

Postpartum depression.

Maybe it's been one-too-many of those 3 a.m. feedings, pretending not to hear the baby wailing in the next room while Marla snores like a freight train. Or the infant world of diaper changing, soft-serve vomit and that slow-healing belly button. Or it could be as simple as the way little Tiffany looks at him so unknowingly, so unaware that he is not just the man who made her mother pregnant. He is Donald Trump.

And so maybe he tried to cure this hangover of parental responsibility with a shot of publicity.

A return to his roots. Out of the nursery and back into the jungle. Time to break out of that constricted, behind-closed-doors world of child rearing and back into the arena of the deal.

Success Story: 1990s. Full occupancy at Trump Plaza. Signature in inch-high letters.

Make it a full page.

Something for the kid's scrapbook.

Poor guy. He's got it bad. The depth of his postpartum depression must be so great that none of his handlers sought to reign him in on this one.

It might have been too emotionally risky for a gentle, "But Donald, you don't own that anymore," line.

Although you'd think he might have remembered it.

In the four years he owned Trump Plaza, the 221-unit project was more than half-empty. And despite international advertising, sales had slowed to a trickle before the banks closed in for the kill.

The place filled up because many of the units were sold at auction — often for less than half of the original asking prices.

You'd think Trump would remember that too, how the banks pressured him into holding an auction of the unsold units, and how he presided over the final indignity of it — like some teenager made to resod his neighbor's front yard after getting caught pulling a lawn job.

One of Florida's great success stories?

Even the ad's picture is misleading.

It shows the words "Trump Plaza" in block letters at the top of the northern tower.

But the words aren't on the building anymore.

Let's not tell Donald, though.

We wouldn't want to get him any more depressed than he already must be.

Man-made disasters: Trump and Limbaugh   103

Rush and Kathryn Rogers Limbaugh take shelter from the rain at St. John Boutique after the Worth Avenue Association's Annual Tree Lighting Ceremony Tuesday. (Meghan McCarthy/The Palm Beach Post)

Limbaugh walks down the aisle again, but No. 4 could be the charm
June 4, 2010

Do I really wish Rush well? I do, I do, I do, I do

Rush Limbaugh is getting married this weekend in Palm Beach, and I hope he doesn't fail.

After all, he is the make-believe president of the alternative-universe United States, and it would be rude to root for failure as he embarks on a new administration of wedding vows.

"I don't want this to work," I could have said, mimicking Limbaugh's wishes of ill will to the nation's real president: "I hope Obama fails. Somebody's gotta say it."

Limbaugh said that wishing for Barack Obama to succeed is OK only if you "want to promote incompetence."

I could have said the same thing about Limbaugh, who is getting married for the fourth time on Saturday.

But I'd rather look for positive signs. And there are some.

For starters, Limbaugh's marriages get longer each time.

The first one to a radio station secretary lasted three years. Then his marriage to a ballpark usherette made it to seven years. And he held on for a full 10 years in his third marriage to an aerobic instructor/radio-show groupie.

This is what we call a trend story in the drive-by media.

So we can deduce that his fourth marriage, to Kathryn Rogers, 33, a West Palm Beach party planner he met at a celebrity golf tournament, might just carry the 59-year-old Limbaugh into his early 70s before he becomes smitten with a cosmetologist, a hat-check girl or a coffee shop barista.

But who knows? Maybe No. 4 will turn out to be the charm. I hope so.

Everybody deserves to be happy. Even Limbaugh.

And when it comes to marriage, nobody's an expert, or has the right to gloat. Marriage is a story that only reveals itself over time. It's an uncharted marathon.

Look at Al and Tipper Gore, a couple who made public kissing seem almost obscene. They're splitting after 40 years, while Bill and Hillary Clinton still manage to make their thing work. Go figure.

Limbaugh couldn't help himself, taking a swipe at Gore's marriage breakup by citing a study that concluded that divorce is bad for the environment, because when people split up, they consume more resources than they did as a couple.

"The environmental wackos have put this notion up there that divorce contributes to global warming," Limbaugh said on his radio show. "And now, here is Mr. Global Warming, a Nobel Peace Prize winner, now contributing to his own crisis."

That's just mean. That would be like me pointing out that Mr. Talent-on-Loan-from-God's fourth marriage is bad for the right-wing religious wackos and their zany notions of "the sanctity of marriage." And that Limbaugh's wedding only sets up the possibility of yet another breakup, adding to his already significant contribution to the divorce crisis.

But I say, screw the religious zealots and their alarmist end-of-the-world rhetoric. Limbaugh deserves another mulligan. He's making steady improvements when it comes to hanging onto wives.

You might even call it change we can believe in.

Pretend-presidential candidate Donald Trump on the stump in Boca Raton. (Gary Coronado/The Palm Beach Post)

The Donald takes his fake run for president to Boca Raton
June 24, 2011

Trump bailout is all about tea, fake sympathy

I'm a softie for happy endings, so it was great news to learn that the South Florida Tea Party will receive a bailout for whining beyond its means.

I had been concerned that the tea partyers' unpaid bill for Boca Raton's services would become a socialized debt to the city. That would have sent the wrong message.

After all, a gathering at Sanborn Square was all about how taxes are too high because spending is excessive. So it would have been a disappointing final chapter of the day if the taxpayers in Boca had to foot the unpaid bill for cops and barricades because the tea party group ran up expenses it couldn't pay for its anti-spending rally.

Instead, Donald Trump, who had been the pretend presidential candidate who headlined the rally, agreed to pay the $6,000 bill to the city.

"Mr. Trump is honored that so many people came to hear him speak on important political and social issues," his adviser Michael

Cohen told Politico. "Mr. Trump does not want any citizen group to be disparaged or burdened for exercising their First Amendment right and has agreed to personally cover the full obligation to the city of Boca Raton."

South Florida Tea Party Chairman Everett Wilkinson optimistically estimated the crowd at the rally at more than 2,000. But Trump's statement this week put the "unexpectedly large number of citizens" attending the rally at more than 5,000.

My guess is that by the time a retelling of the day makes it into the next Trump autobiography (suggested title: I Really Could Have Been President), the Boca crowd will have swelled to 20,000.

As for the "important political and social issues" Trump discussed that day ... well, I confess, I'm stumped.

I was there. He spent a lot of time questioning President Obama's citizenship (pure nonsense) and talking crazy (seizing Middle East oil) as he rambled on about what he'd do once he was elected president – which was not the job he was really angling for.

It appears that Trump's game was using a lot of simpletons to boost his status as a reality TV star.

Forget Washington and Jefferson. He was trying to follow in the footsteps of Snooki and the Kardashians.

Trump's fake campaign for president helped the ratings of his *Celebrity Apprentice* show at a time when he had to negotiate a new two-year contract for the program.

And the end of Trump's "campaign" for president coincided with the ink drying on that contract.

Trump will be making $65 million a year from the new deal, a raise that makes him the highest-paid reality TV star in America, the *New York Post* reported.

So paying a few thousand dollars to settle a tea party bill is the least he could do to help out all those imaginary patriots who waved their "Trump 2012" signs at him as he indulged their deepest Obama fantasies for his own gain.

"Thank you, Donald Trump," wrote a woman commenting on this newspaper's website about Trump's offer to pay the bill. "The rally was great and people who did not attend missed a real opportunity to learn more about our nation and what it stands for."

I think P.T. Barnum would agree.

**Rush ridicules 'environmental wackos,'
but ends up laying an egg**
March 17, 2010

Limbaugh needs tutorial in turtle ways

Rush Limbaugh's great at using satire to make a point.

He's a master at using humor to show the absurdity of those wacko (fill in the blank), who are ruining this country by impinging on the rights of the decent, hardworking real Americans. Like him. It was in that spirit that Limbaugh took a full-page ad in *The Palm Beach Post* to declare himself the executive director of the Turtle Preservation Society of Palm Beach.

"Welcome back to our beaches, turtles and hatchlings," his ad said. "The lights are off in eager anticipation of your arrival in May."

Being satire, the point wasn't to applaud sea turtle advocates, but to mock them.

This should come as no surprise. Limbaugh probably needed a breather from ridiculing human health care to dabble in the ridicule of turtle health care, which he finds taxing due to the constraints it puts on his landscape lighting options at his oceanfront Palm Beach home.

He probably just sees turtle lights as a government-sanctioned health insurance program for marine life.

From March 1 to Oct. 31 each year, oceanfront homeowners are reminded to make accommodations for nesting turtles.

Or, as Limbaugh put it so eloquently on his radio show, "The theory from environmental nut case wackos is that lights on the beach distract the hatchlings and cause them not to go to the ocean but inland."

By "environmental nut case wackos," I think he means all marine biologists.

But that's a small hurdle to jump in Limbaugh's world.

Ridiculing science when it gets in the way of selfish motives is already in the playbook. So it's a cinch to do the turtle equivalent of global warming hoax-mongering.

In Limbaugh's ad, he defends his treasured landscape lighting by proposing two revisions to science:

The first is that he's being made to modify his lights in March, when the turtles don't come ashore until May. And the second is that turtle lighting is silly because turtles come ashore to lay their eggs during the day. He's got the photographic proof!

Instead of buying the ad, Limbaugh might have been better off going to Turtle Day at the Gumbo Limbo Nature Center in Boca Raton on Saturday. The nature center counts turtle nests, rehabilitates injured turtles and educates the public about the three species of sea turtles that nest on South Florida's beaches.

Limbaugh could have learned that the endangered leatherback turtles start nesting in March, and that turtles almost always come ashore at night to lay their eggs.

Even better, Gumbo Limbo has a display of four turtle-friendly lighting options Limbaugh could use for his backyard lighting.

"Why care about turtles?" I asked Gumbo Limbo's development director, Mike Zewe.

"They've been around for 150 million years and the impact we've had over the past 60 years has depleted them," he said. "How would you like to explain to your grandkids that they can't see a sea turtle because of what we did?"

CHAPTER 10
Man-made disasters, Part II
The Election of 2000

County voters wander the wrong way in presidential vote
Nov. 9, 2000

To mess up is natural, so revote right in line

We need a do-over.

Excuse me, America. Sorry we have to meet like this. We here in Palm Beach County were hoping to take the national stage under better circumstances. But we have a problem that needs your

Man-made disasters, Part II: The Election of 2000

attention. Even if it makes us look, um, silly.

You see . . . we'd like to vote again for the president.

I know. I know. This is highly unusual.

We understand the idea is everybody gets one crack at it.

But we screwed up on Tuesday. And this, being the land of golf, entitles us to a mulligan.

Here's why. We were confused.

We often are. We sometimes park cars in swimming pools and get lost on the roads despite signs with letters big enough to read from the Space Shuttle.

So it's no wonder that some of the condo vote ended up going to Pat Buchanan.

We were trying to vote for Al Gore. And I know we should have just followed the arrow that led from Gore's name on the ballot to the hole we had to punch.

But we got lost on the way. It happens. We were moving our hand across the page, and we wandered, punching No. 4 on the ballot instead of No. 5.

It's a lot like that mistake between the brake and the gas pedals.

The No. 4 is like the gas, and the No. 5 is like the brake.

We were trying to hit the brake, and we hit the gas.

And this time, instead of crashing the strip shopping center, we crashed the election for the president of the United States.

Oops. Sorry.

Let's back up and try again.

Not only is the election of the next president on the line. With George W. Bush and Gore separated by 1,784 votes across the state, changing most of the county's 3,407 votes for Buchanan could determine the winner of the election.

But nearly as important, it's embarrassing to us.

We don't want to have anything to do with Buchanan, who couldn't get hundreds of condo votes even if he showed up on Election Day with a tractor-trailer full of free corned beef sandwiches.

I know what you're thinking: If the layout of the ballot caused some Gore voters to choose Buchanan by mistake, maybe it also caused Buchanan voters to choose Gore in error.

Wrong. You don't hear Buchanan people complaining. That's

because they didn't have trouble voting for their guy. All those Buchanan people have great aim. I think it has something to do with the guns.

They were punching bull's-eyes. And we were voting for a guy with a soft spot for Hitler.

This can't happen. So here's the deal.

Hold a retake of the election in Palm Beach County, in which only the people who voted Tuesday will be eligible to vote again.

Make it in a couple of weeks.

That will give the candidates and their campaigns time to come here and promise us a whole new bunch of things they won't be able to deliver.

Maybe Palm Beach County seniors can negotiate their own prescription plan with the Democrats. The Republicans could cough up Wayne Newton for a free concert at the Kravis.

Either party is more than welcome to pay for the bullet train.

So, come on down.

We've got lots of things we'd like you to do for us. Boca Raton needs a new high school. Palm Tran needs covered shelters. And how about a tax break on bingo earnings?

We'll tell the gate guard to let you in. Bring lots of sandwiches.

And this time when we vote, we promise to pay more attention.

Katherine Harris and Carol Roberts: Two inspiring 'candidates' emerge
Nov. 16, 2000

Don't turn out the lights, because the parties are not over

Attention debutantes. Calling all Junior Leaguers, and Barbie collectors.

Rally for Katherine Harris in West Palm Beach this afternoon. Heels optional. She needs your help.

"This is an important message from Republican headquarters," the recorded announcement said to phones across Palm Beach County.

Man-made disasters, Part II: The Election of 2000

"Please join us for a rally in support of Katherine Harris and the Florida rule of law."

The Republicans' message went out a couple hours before Harris, looking very much like the flight attendant who doesn't give you the whole can of soda, announced that after careful consideration — hardy, har-har — she wasn't going to accept any more hand counts of ballots.

C'mon, Republicans. This is your Jesse Jackson rally today. The citrus-magnate's granddaughter needs your help. The party fem-bot is under attack.

So repeat after me, "We shall overlook . . . We shall overlook."

I love this election. Finally, we get to support two people who are far more inspiring than George W. Bush and Al Gore.

I'm talking, of course, about the two party women who have emerged as the bloodied foot soldiers for their respective armies.

For the Republicans, we have Harris, who reeks with a sort of let-them-eat-cake demeanor that must make trust-fund hearts beat with pride.

And on the Democrats' side, we have our very own Carol Roberts, who has in the past week been transformed into the Condo Countess, a woman who seems so ready to announce new numbers that she'll probably end up as a bingo barker when this is done.

Both women are dangerous.

Harris has shown herself to have the determination of a department store cosmetics section spritzer lady.

And Roberts is the person you can count on to elbow her way to the last gallon of milk at Publix.

Never before have two women better embodied their parties.

You look at Harris, and you can see the vast emptiness there, and the need for the handlers who walk her back and forth to her podium, and answer all the questions that go beyond her script.

You can imagine her sitting in some inner sanctum, taking an emery board to her nails while the lawyers write the heartfelt reasoning she will be reading.

Roberts follows the script of her party too, but in the hurly-burly way of an old-style machine politician. Nobody needs to tell her how to throw punches. And every day she looks less like the county's arts-loving county commissioner, and more like an irritated condo commando who is deciding whether to remove soap from the clubhouse showers for safety reasons.

Both parties have tried their best to boot Harris and Roberts from the election process. The Democrats have used the courts in an effort to circumvent Harris' authority. And the Republicans charged Wednesday that Roberts should be removed from the canvassing board, accusing her of "twisting, bending, poking and purposefully manipulating ballots."

But both women have parried the attacks and held their ground.

When Harris was putting fresh blood in the water Wednesday night with her announcement, Roberts was asleep, turning down an invitation to be on Larry King for a chance to get a good night's sleep and fight afresh today.

No telling what Roberts will do today. But you can count on it being nasty and to the point. And before this election is over, the only thing that's certain is that both these women will toe their party's line to the end.

'The Palm Beach judge is here': Chuck Burton's visit to the Supreme Court
Dec. 2, 2000

A man of the people in America's capital

It's getting close to midnight, but Chuck Burton is too restless to walk through the hotel's revolving door and call it a night.

Instead, he heads up the street, past Washington D.C.'s glowing, silent Capitol building toward the candles flickering outside the U.S. Supreme Court. In the morning, the court will hear lawyers argue over the election recounts — his recounts — in a case called Bush vs. Palm Beach County Canvassing Board.

Burton has never been to the Supreme Court, and he has never imagined living a life that has made a lower-court judge in Palm Beach County one of the more recognizable judges in America.

He lights a cigarette, just another guy in jeans and ski jacket, a spectator — finally — to the story.

Outside the Supreme Court, hundreds of people are camped out, preparing to spend the night in hopes of a getting a ringside seat to history in the morning.

Man-made disasters, Part II: The Election of 2000

They look up from their sleeping bags and tents. It's dark. They look twice, sometimes walking alongside him for a few steps, just to make sure.

Seeing Burton standing there is like seeing an apparition and is a validation of the idea that average people can play great roles in democracy.

"Hey, you're the judge," Stephanie Olsen, 36, of Alexandria, Va., says as Burton walks by.

"I was going to send him flowers," Olsen says excitedly to her friend, "and here he is!"

Burton stops, gives his sleepy-eyed smile and chats.

"You people are our heroes," Olsen says to him. "Especially you, the way people were always hanging over your shoulders."

Burton has been out of Palm Beach County for about five hours, and he's beginning to find that he has become one of the more popular guys in America.

He's still trying to work out why.

Maybe it's his willingness to keep a sense of humor in a tough situation, to deflect tension with a smile or an eye roll. Or maybe it's just pity, the recognition across the land that nobody in their right mind should have to stare at 462,644 ballots.

Then again, it might just be all that TV time.

"I feel like you're part of my living room," says Moses Rojas, 23, who is 22nd in a public spectator line that began forming a day before the oral arguments.

"I don't know how you're still awake," legal assistant Rebecca Freedman, 22, says to Burton.

Lauren Hamilton, a social science researcher, asks if he's here to wait in line.

"No, actually, I have a ticket," Burton says, sounding apologetic to the people who were planning to shiver away the night for a chance to spend three minutes inside the courtroom Friday.

Burton got a seat from Bruce Rogow, a constitutional lawyer who represented the canvassing board and pulled strings with the court's marshals to get an extra ticket for Burton in a spectator section.

"Don't apologize," Hamilton tells Burton. "You deserve to be inside. You have our proxy."

Chuck Burton, the people's judge. It's a mantle that fits him well.

114 Writing Like a Taller Person: The Best of Frank Cerabino

In a partisan struggle, where people's positions could be determined simply by looking for an R or D after their names, Burton has been seen as an oddball, a guy who was trying to play it down the middle while people were pulling him apart from both sides.

So as word spreads around the building that "the Palm Beach judge is here," people wander over to Burton to talk, pose for a photo with him or get his autograph.

Burton, who has been in the company of scowling lawyers for three weeks, seems to relish some benign human interaction.

"I should have brought some chads," he jokes.

"You have a good sense of humor," says Jordan Usdan, 19, a George Washington University sophomore from Broward County. "You ought to have a talk show."

"Judge Chuckie," Burton says.

Earlier in the evening, while finishing his dinner at a Capitol Hill bistro, a cluster of people were looking at him and debating whether it was really him. One worked up the nerve to ask.

"Would it help you if I assume the position?" Burton said, pretending to hold an imaginary ballot card over his head.

Carol Roberts, Chuck Burton and Theresa LePore look for hanging chads, as attorneys surround them. (Lannis Waters/The Palm Beach Post)

Man-made disasters, Part II: The Election of 2000

Burton wonders how long it will last.

"I'd like to know when I'll get my life back," he says.

He goes to his local Walgreens and the seniors waiting for flu shots ask, "So, are we going to win, judge?" He flies to Washington and, bingo, his ticket has mysteriously been upgraded by the travel agency to first class, no extra charge.

The businessman on the plane looks at him in his jeans and says, "I hope you're not going to wear that in court tomorrow."

He sits in his hotel lobby, sipping coffee, and strangers line up to tell him "thanks."

"You did a terrific job," Michael Holland, a labor lawyer from Chicago tells him. "I appreciate your evenhandedness, and this is coming from a liberal Democrat."

Burton thought he had a thankless job. But he's beginning to think differently. *Time* magazine has put him down as "a winner" in this national soap opera, and the man on the street seems to agree.

Brandon Danz, a Republican club member at Millersville University in Lancaster, Pa., walks alongside Burton, nervously waiting for his chance to say something.

"I'm a Republican, but you did a pretty fair job," Danz says. "Although the eye rolls were too much."

Adam Freudberg, 17, the president of his McLean, Va., Young Democrats Club, pulls out a sample Palm Beach County ballot that he bought on e-Bay for $22.

As Burton autographs it, Freudberg tells his friend, "What's the odds of this? He was just on Larry King two nights ago!"

Denise Dytrych, the county attorney who advised the canvassing board, also traveled to Washington with Burton. But she didn't have the celebrity Burton seemed to have. Still, she enjoyed watching everyone's reaction to him.

"He's the dimpled chad judge," Dytrych explained to the hotel clerk who couldn't figure out why other people in the lobby were making a fuss over Burton.

On Friday, Dytrych stood outside the Supreme Court building with constitutional lawyer Beverly Pohl at 6 a.m., waiting for one of the spots in a lawyers' room, where they could listen to but not see the oral arguments.

Burton, meanwhile, took a cab to the court with Rogow, the

constitutional lawyer, who had made 11 oral arguments himself in front of the court and had told Burton what to expect.

"I wish I could take my camera," Burton said as he got ready to go.

As he and Rogow walked past the line of shivering lawyers waiting on the side of the building, the lawyers turned to look at Burton. Some of them, like Georgetown Law Professor Paul Rothstein, shook Burton's hand and told him he did a good job.

A Dutch television crew spotted Burton and ran after him for a quick interview.

After the court session, Burton walked out a side door, where a battery of cameras and microphones waited. All around the building, lawyers and activists such as Al Sharpton were talking about grave constitutional issues and heroic struggles.

Burton stood in the half-circle of cameras, and someone asked if he had any regrets over the recount.

"I missed my daughter's birthday," Burton said.

As he walked away, a man came up to him and patted him on the back.

"That's the most important thing," he told Burton. "Your daughter's birthday."

Burton walked away from the building toward the fringes of the crowd.

Somebody shouted, "It's the Palm Beach guy!"

There would be more photos to pose for, autographs to sign. Then he was free, trying to make his flight to Tallahassee, where he was certain to be criticized in court today for doing too much, or too little, depending who was asking the questions.

But at least he had this day, this time where the most junior of judges had a seat in the highest court of the land. It was something to remember.

"I sat next to Ted Koppel," Burton said.

And yes, Koppel knew him, too.

CHAPTER 11
Marriage (and divorce)
Palm-Beach-County style

Palm Beach's first lady of family court returns to her roots
Dec. 4, 1992

Love is a many splintered thing for Roxanne Pulitzer

If the philosopher Rene Descartes were alive to ponder the Palm Beach social scene, he might sum up Roxanne Pulitzer's latest move this way:

Alimonyum, ergo sum.

I divorce, therefore I am.

Pulitzer, Palm Beach's first lady of family court, has returned to her roots after a brief experiment with something called a husband.

The bonds of Pulitzer's marriage to John Haggin Jr. are "irretrievably broken," the two-page court document says.

I'm not sure how "broken" a marriage can be after 48 days.

Marriage vows Oct. 16. Divorce papers Dec. 2.

I've had haircuts that lasted longer.

Even if Pulitzer's marriage were measured in dog time, it still comes to less than a year.

It was, by any standard, a microwave marriage. Till death — or some bad vibes — do us part.

She had just enough time to fit in a 6-carat diamond ring, one Donahue appearance about her marital bliss, and then a brief separation.

They gave each other some of the best hours of their lives, but it just didn't work out. At least they'll always have November.

Roxanne's divorce petition showed a humorous touch: "No children were born of the marriage."

(I'll let you know if a zygote custody battle develops.)

The divorce is good news for the county. It returns Roxanne to her natural state, preserving one of our most prolific resources.

Elsewhere, production is measured in things such as bauxite, soybeans or bituminous coal.

But in Palm Beach County, it's the perils of Roxanne. I checked the newspaper's computer files for stories mentioning her:

Year	Stories
1989	26
1990	38
1991	43
1992	32

That's major-league consistency.

At first, this guy Haggin looked like he had potential, like he could improve Roxanne's game. Haggin's fashionably underemployed. And there's $200 million buried under his family tree.

But then the happy couple announced on Donahue that their marriage would probably cost Haggin his share of the family coin.

"Gave up $200 million for love" flashed on the TV screen.

And that's when you first realized that this guy might be a taco shy of the combination plate.

Poor Roxanne.

Haggin's a Military Trail kind of guy. He likes to sit at home and drink beer out of a keg he keeps in his living room.

"It's easier than going to the kitchen," he once explained.

Burp.

You can get the picture. Pretty soon, Roxanne would be seen in a polyester pantsuit at Winn-Dixie, buying an econo-sized case of Vienna sausages for her man. And then she'd be just like us.

Ten years cultivating her celebrity divorcee status down the drain. Ahead, nothing but the oblivion that flourishes on the west side of the Intracoastal Waterway.

End of story.

"Palm Beach County eyes bauxite production," the headlines

Marriage (and divorce) Palm-Beach-County style   119

would start saying.

But fortunately, Roxanne pulled herself out of this nose dive in time. Or maybe it was Haggin who woke up screaming in terror as, "Gave up $200 million for love," flashed before his eyes.

There's no shortage of creative explanations why the Haggin-Pulitzer bond was formed and broken.

And that's good. It means more Roxanne stories. It means she might even top last year's production.

Life is returning to normal, as if this whole embarrassing episode never happened.

The divorce is set to be wrapped up next week in a brief, uncontested court hearing.

Roxanne's back in Palm Beach, living in the Colony Hotel. She's already been seen with her old boyfriend, Jean de la Moussaye, an almost-life-size French Count who has the good sense to practice his underemployment in Palm Beach.

Welcome back, Roxanne. You scared us.

Send some smoke signals up from The Colony to tell us your plans.

One puff for Geraldo; two for Sally Jesse; three for Oprah.

Shedding a grand tier: Love blossoms at the Kravis Center
Sept. 24, 1993

Ushers plan a walk down the aisle

So I'm sitting at usher school at the Kravis Center — don't laugh. It's eight hours and ends with a 90-question multiple choice test. It's easier to get a driver license.

And the guy next to me says, "This is where they got engaged, right here."

Sunday. Before the Flying Karamozov Brothers matinee. He had more than a D-cell flashlight in his hands, and she said "Yes."

Just like that. Lifetime season tickets.

Love? It didn't mention anything about love in the 34-page "New and Improved Kravis Center Usher Manual."

All along, I thought it was just a matter of memorizing where the fire alarm boxes are. Or remembering that the grand tier has eight boxes, and the mezzanine has 10. That you press "3U" for the balcony elevator. And it's odd seat numbers to the left, even to the right. Or that there's no Row "I" in the orchestra. Or that you never say "ticket duplication," but rather "a ticket situation."

But what about the situation of ushers Tom Noe and Jeanne Netwig?

A Kravis crush. A mezzanine amour. A second-time-around aisle walk for a couple of volunteer aisle patrollers.

It's enough to make you shed a grand tier, or feel a warm spot in the orchestra pit of your stomach.

But it's not addressed in the manual. Unless you count: "The Center wants very much to make the usher program as satisfying, and rewarding to our volunteers as we possibly can."

And what will become of this Kravis romance?

"I would love to get married there," said Netwig. "I can see myself coming down the grand staircase."

Which connects the loge, not the grand tier, to the orchestra level. (An usher-test question.)

And what would a Kravis wedding of ushers be like?

Ticketron invitations? A guest list verified by (another test term) a drop count? A receiving line of red-blazered, white-shirted people bearing crossed flashlights? Will the house lights be blinked before the ceremony begins? And will the usher-guests still be required to park on the garage roof and show up two hours early?

Somehow, "please watch your step" doesn't sound appropriate at a wedding.

Noe, a 50-year-old yacht service operator, and Netwig, a 46-year-old mail carrier, are relative youngsters in the retiree-dominated ushering corps. But will the news of their flowering romance be the siren call to every condo lothario with a free night and a roaming eye for untethered grandmas?

Could an outbreak of loge lizards plague the Kravis?

House manager Marc Engel, who teaches the usher course, has never had to contemplate these kind of questions.

But he's no stranger to usher love.

"I married an usher," he said.

Marriage (and divorce) Palm-Beach-County style

It was an usher he met when he was the house manager at a Nashville theater.

Noe and Netwig were just a couple of strangers among the volunteers who milled in the lobby a year ago before the Miami City Ballet's Jewels performance.

Noe was a Thursday usher, but volunteered on that Sunday night because the theater was shorthanded. After he met Netwig, he started volunteering for Sundays. And Netwig started showing up Thursdays. And a volunteer courtship began for these two divorcees.

"We've shared some intimate moments at the Kravis," Netwig said. "I get sentimental just thinking about it."

And while they were preparing to usher for Sunday's show, the beginning of their second volunteer season, Noe guided her to the balcony.

"It's such a romantic view," he said.

He handed her a brown paper bag and asked Netwig to fish inside it for the little maroon box.

"I said, 'Well, being as this is such a special place for us, I think this would be appropriate.'"

"She took so long to say anything," he said.

"I couldn't speak," she said.

Life's finest production number, played once again on the only stage that really matters.

Another reason to be thankful for the Kravis.

A sad tale of a Tyco exec and his waitress/mistress/wife
Feb. 15, 2008

Love story has bitter ending for jailed CEO

Valentine's Day is over. So let's get right to a heartbreaking tale of love gone wrong.

Karen Kozlowski had one of those storybook romances, the kind most of us only dream about. You know the one: Attractive 30-something, twice-divorced waitress at a seafood restaurant meets corporate pirate who is 15 years older, already married and has the looks that could make him the stunt double for Lex Luthor,

Superman's nemesis.

Cupid, take out your bow!

Am I leaving something out? Oh, yeah. He makes about $100 million a year.

You have all the elements for a Disney princess movie right there. OK, you'd have to tweak the thieving corporate scoundrel part, edit out the first wife and make him look more like Superman and less like the Superman villain.

But other than those minor changes, Dennis Kozlowski, the former chief executive officer of Tyco, was quite a Prince Charming, and his waitress-turned-mistress-turned-wife was quite an impressive "merger and acquisition," as a person in Kozlowski's line of work might say.

Kozlowski got rich transforming a modest New Hampshire company into a corporate giant.

Tyco moved into an office building in Boca Raton, and Kozlowski and the former waitress moved to a mansion in The Sanctuary development in Boca.

But even $100 million a year isn't enough sometimes. So Kozlowski used Tyco's money as a bottomless piggy bank: money he could take and never repay.

Prosecutors would later estimate that Kozlowski and his chief financial officer glommed about $600 million from the company.

But let's get back to the tender love story. Dennis and Karen married on Antigua in May 2001.

A month later, he flew her to Sardinia for her very special 40th birthday party, a $2 million bash for which Tyco paid half. Jimmy Buffett performed, models posed poolside in their togas and an ice sculpture of Michelangelo's David dispensed a trickle of vodka from the end of ... um, well, let's just say in the Disney version it would be changed to the statue's finger.

The newlyweds seemed to have a charmed life, including a $30 million apartment in New York with a $6,000 shower curtain. But a clumsy attempt to avoid paying sales tax on art brought a spotlight to Dennis Kozlowski that would lead to trouble.

By the time the New York district attorney was done, Kozlowski was convicted of 22 counts of grand larceny, securities fraud and other charges.

Karen wept at his conviction in 2005. Kozlowski lost his appeal and began serving at least eight years in prison, where he earns $1 a day.

Can you guess how this love story ends?

In the Disney version, Karen would go back to serving the Fisherman's Platter, biding her time until the day her Lex Luthor walks in, leaner and wiser from his days behind bars.

He'd get on his knees during the dinner rush and beg her to take him back so they could start from scratch. No $6,000 shower curtains this time, he'd say.

Everybody in the restaurant would applaud. She'd wipe her eyes and toss off her apron, and they'd share a Lake Worth apartment with Guatemalan laborers, penniless but in love.

But like I said, this turned out to be a tale of love gone wrong.

Kozlowski went to prison, the government went after his money and Karen filed for divorce. Her lawyer complained that Dennis Kozlowski needs to hurry up and pay the rest of the $167 million he owes the government, so Karen could get half of what's left from their marital assets as well as alimony "whether permanent, periodic, lump sum, rehabilitative, 'bridge-the-gap,' or any hybrid thereof."

Sounds like she's just settling for money. Who could have predicted that such a great love story would end on a note like this?

The wedding of a condemned man and his Lake Worth bride
Jan. 7, 1994

No-touch nuptials the social event on Death Row

A new kind of electricity is running through Florida's Death Row these days as that charming cloistered retreat prepares for the main event of this year's Starke social season.

The current sensation is the upcoming nuptials of Wanda Eads, 50, of Lake Worth, and her betrothed, Frank Valdes, 31, who took up involuntary permanent residence in Starke three years ago. Security bells will ring on the morning of Jan. 21, as the wedding party makes its way to the quaint maximum-security, glass-partitioned visitation room.

As events go, this will be one of the hardest to attend. The paparazzi will be kept away with the help of barbed wire fences. No photos.

"It's a very private situation," said Rhonda Horler, the warden's social director.

It promises to be an affair in which details count, right down to the body frisking.

The theme is "no touch."

The bride will wear a cream-colored suit and hold a bouquet that has been scanned for metal objects. The groom will wear the traditional prison blue, but the release of handcuffs during the service will add that special bit of panache.

The ushers will wear uniforms.

The best man, Sal Tarantola, the owner of Prison Connection Bus Service, says much yet needs to be done to figure out exactly where he should stand.

"I don't even know how I'm supposed to get the rings to the guy," he said. "What am I supposed to do, slip the rings through the glass?"

The bride-to-be says she will only accept the wedding ring from the hand of her condemned man.

"I'm not letting a guard put the ring on me," she said.

Etiquette books are silent on this point.

The wedding service will be performed by the groom's criminal defense attorney Joseph Karp.

There will be no appeal.

The groom's death sentence for the murder of a corrections officer in West Palm Beach seven years ago has already been upheld by the Florida Supreme Court. He's running out of second opinions.

The bride-to-be is upbeat. Her home phone answering machine says, "You've reached Frank and Wanda's place."

Frank's just not at home for the rest of his life — and seven additional lives, according to his sentence.

But love, in this case, is said to be eternal.

"Frank's treated me well," Wanda said. "We're on the same spiritual level. I have never cheated on him, and I never will."

The couple says God has brought them together.

A Supreme Being could not be reached for comment.

The marriage should be simple, if not long.

Marital transgressions from the groom, who spends all day alone in an 8-by-10 cell, are not expected. And if the wedding sours, the special conditions of this union would obviate any need for the wife to hire a hit man.

The state's already provided one.

The bride-to-be fell in love with her beau after he was arrested for the shooting death of a corrections officer. One of her friends has married a convicted bludgeon murderer.

Starke social climbing at its finest.

The bride-to-be's first three husbands were not condemned murderers. It's uncertain whether any of them are receiving counseling or calling daytime talk-show producers to pitch a show titled: "My wife left me for a guy on Death Row."

The bride-to-be says she has already heard from Connie Chung's producer and a man from the William Morris Agency who wants to talk about a movie deal.

The bride-to-be hopes to work out the logistical uncertainties of the "no contact" ceremony this weekend.

Karp suggested a twist on the traditional Jewish service that features the stomping of a glass.

"Maybe we can get a glazier in there to cut through the glass between them," he said.

If not, Karp's not sure what he'll say.

Somehow, "I pronounce you man and wife, now you may kiss the glass," doesn't have a ring to it.

Horler, the warden's social director, says there will be no cake, no dancing, no music and no reception afterward. (In other words, the affair will have a Baptist flavor to it.)

Honeymoon plans are nonexistent. In lieu of gifts, particularly toasters, the couple is accepting pardons in the name of the groom.

As far as the wedding vows, the two lovebirds will be writing their own.

Horler says they won't be required to include the traditional line about "till death do us part."

"I imagine they could forgo that," she said.

County's confusing bridal requirement washes out with the tide
June 13, 2007

Lifeguard rule for beach weddings has false ring to it

I need to clear something up for the tourists.

If you're coming to Palm Beach County to have a wedding ceremony on the beach, you do not need to hire a lifeguard. I repeat: Weddings on the beach in Palm Beach County do not require a lifeguard.

Yes, this needs to be said.

Because if you happened to be perusing the Palm Beach County Convention and Visitors Bureau website, as I was, you would have seen that Question No. 11 among those visitors frequently ask is whether they may have beach weddings. And here's the tourist bureau's answer, in part:

"Ceremonies may last no longer than fifteen minutes and must have a lifeguard on duty."

The 15-minute time limit was strange enough, but to heap a lifeguard on top of that was testing the limits of credulity.

Could it be? How much ceremonial protocol and perilous water play could a wedding party accomplish in such a short time?

My first inclination was to believe that the county really did require lifeguards to be standing by for action at beach weddings, because, well, it sounded like something the county would do.

But I had a tougher time imagining a lifeguard's duties during a beach wedding.

Maybe something like this: You'd be in the middle of reciting "If Thou Must Love Me" by Elizabeth Barrett Browning, when a shrill whistle pierces the air.

All eyes turn to that shirtless guy with the six-pack abs and the big glob of white sunblock on his nose, as he stands nearby with a coil of rope at his feet, motioning repeatedly with his arms to bring the bridesmaids in another foot from the high tide mark.

Or that maybe when the bride's old boyfriend shows up unannounced, the duty lifeguard gets to yell, "Shark!"

OK, maybe not. But there were certainly some disturbing

questions to answer. For example:

Once the groom says "I do," does the lifeguard stop trying to save him? And how many brides end up with a life-saving float tossed over their heads following the ceremonial pronouncement that she should be given the ring?

So I called some professionals, starting with Chaplain Bob Walker, who specializes in performing beach weddings in Palm Beach and Broward counties.

"I'd never heard of lifeguards," Walker said. "Maybe that's in case the bride wants to dunk the groom."

Ian Garman, a lifeguard at Riviera Beach Ocean Rescue, said the oceanfront beach at Singer Island is a frequent site for wedding ceremonies, but the lifeguards aren't involved.

"The people in those weddings are dressed in clothes, and nobody gets wet," Garman said. "They don't even stand in the wet sand. They keep to the dry sand."

The alleged 15-minute time limit was also a mystery.

"It's a public beach," said Benjamin Smith, the chief supervisor of Lake Worth Ocean Rescue. "You can have an eight-hour wedding on the beach if you want. Just as long as you pay the parking."

A few cities, such as Palm Beach and Boca Raton, require permits for beach weddings, and there are some restrictions because of turtle egg nests and bonfires. But Palm Beach County is apparently more open to beach weddings than you might imagine after reading the tourist advisory.

So I called the Palm Beach County Convention and Visitors Bureau and found out that the information about lifeguards at quickie beach weddings was news to them, too.

"Thanks for proofing our site," said Dale Carlson, a spokeswoman for the bureau.

Carlson looked into the matter, and discovered the information about lifeguards was wrong.

"We got that information from somebody," she said. "But we don't know who."

CHAPTER 12
Political sideshows
Public servants of note

Palm Beach County commissioners stalled in rush to the buffet line
May 19, 1995

Politicos dealt poetic justice in stuck elevator

I feel terrible for our county commissioners.

To be trapped the way they were in an elevator at the new courthouse. For half an hour. With each other.

I shudder just thinking about it.

To be trapped with Commissioner Burt Aaronson alone would be traumatizing enough.

But then to throw in the rest of the crowd — Mary, Carol, Maude, Warren and Ken (as Gilligan).

Oh, the horror.

It happened moments after the ceremonial cutting of the ribbon on the $180 million courthouse in downtown West Palm Beach.

The ceremony was at ground level. The free food was on the 11th floor.

The race was on.

County Commissioner Carol Roberts led the way.

This comes as no surprise. Roberts has always been a blue-chipper when it comes to county travel.

Just a couple months ago, County Commissioner Mary McCarty characterized Roberts as an expert freeloader during a heated hallway debate over an Italy boondoggle.

Political sideshows: Public servants of note

So I can imagine that when it comes to beating the crowd to a free champagne buffet, Roberts must be regarded by her colleagues as a bit of an E.F. Hutton figure: When Roberts talks, people listen.

So while the 500 other spectators were getting bottlenecked at the public elevators, Roberts pulled a flanking maneuver.

She headed for a freight elevator with five other commissioners and 11 other local movers and shakers in tow.

Only County Commissioner Karen Marcus had the good fortune of being delayed enough to miss the ill-fated lift.

Something happened along the way to the 11th floor. The would-be scarfers got stuck.

The door in the elevator wouldn't open, and the emergency phone in the elevator car hadn't been connected yet. Even Commissioner Warren Newell's cellphone wouldn't work.

The commissioners have been reticent in discussing what went on inside that elevator car for those 30 minutes.

I can understand why.

For Roberts' sake, it's a good thing her colleagues weren't still clutching their golden scissors from the ribbon-cutting ceremony.

The party began in the courthouse without the commissioners. Nobody searched for them. The other partiers didn't even pay attention to the constant ringing of the elevator's emergency bell.

It must have crushed the commissioners' spirits. And Aaronson must have crushed everything else.

The courthouse, with its construction delays and cost overruns, had always been a rock around their necks. And now it was entombing them, while free food and champagne were being wolfed down just outside their reach.

The commissioners were in politician hell.

And even after they were eventually saved, did they get the nurturing support of their community?

No.

"Where's a good welder when you need one?" seemed to be a popular response to their predicament inside the elevator car.

The effects of an incident like this can be enormous, both to them and the community.

(Note to editors: We need to check whether the county bond rating improved for a half-hour.)

Atheists throughout the county were deeply shaken by the news of the elevator mishap.

"I used to believe the world was a series of random circumstances," one said, "but this smacks of divine intervention."

And to think, for a half-hour, the county was on the bubble. We had lost our ability to legislate:

There was no way to approve another strip shopping center during that time.

No way to issue a tax or a proclamation. No way to respond to the latest request for a handout from the Atlanta Braves and Montreal Expos.

We were a ship without a rudder. Al Haig could have moved here and declared himself in charge. We could have been attacked by Martin County.

On the other hand, at least the 500 other courthouse guests didn't get to the 11th floor and find that the munchies and champagne had already been ravaged by their elected representatives.

The county is treating the incident seriously. It's looking for worldly explanations.

But guess what? The elevator works fine now.

So it looks as if "God's will" still has the inside track. It reminds me of an old biblical saying I just made up:

Theyith who try to glommeth the hors d'oeuvreths, shall inherith the freight elevator while it's stucketh.

Port commissioners weigh in on colleague's weight-loss clinic tab
Jan. 3, 1996

She lost, we lose: Portly official sheds fat on us

Local politicians always talk about taking the fat out of government, but few take those words as literally as Linda Weiss has.

Public money is being spent to send Weiss, a Port of Palm Beach commissioner, to a weight-loss clinic. Money well spent, I say.

According to the latest tally, she's spent $2,070 for "treatment" at a Jupiter clinic and has lost a whopping 8 pounds!

In unenlightened times, you might have expected that Weiss would pay for her own body sculpting. But fortunately, we've progressed to the point where politicians can find a way to burn body flab by burning public money.

And so, a month after Weiss began shedding pounds for the public good, she successfully got fellow commissioners to retroactively include weight-loss treatment as part of the self-insured health coverage for port employees.

Her colleagues took a brief respite from their blabber about being fiscally conservative to hail Weiss' $258-per-pound indulgence as public money well invested.

"Peak condition means peak performance," was how Commissioner Steve Schwack put it.

Only one commissioner seemed mystified — the biggest of them all, Michael Brown.

"I need to lose more weight than the rest of them," said Brown, a former football offensive lineman for Purdue University.

But Brown won't be submitting weight clinic bills to the port.

"It's not right," Brown said. "We shouldn't have to pay for cosmetic procedures for port commissioners. Why should taxpayers pay for port commissioners to lose weight?"

Peak performance, Michael. Peak performance.

We want our elected officials to be in good shape so they can . . . so they can . . . Help me out, Commissioner Brown. You're a port commissioner. What do port commissioners do that requires them to be in peak physical condition?

"I suppose that when you're shuttling from airport to airport . . ." he began.

Aha! Now, you've got it.

Boondoggle junkets. Free trips around the world. Getting wined and dined by tourism people. Packing away platters of free food.

If you're not careful, all that free travel and scarfing can put a few pounds on you.

And if you're already overweight, you might be saddled with guilt the next time you're traveling at somebody else's expense. You might hesitate before cleaning up your plate, or you may be too winded to race across the terminal to your next connecting flight.

You may be, as Commissioner Schwack might put it, in less than "peak condition" to enjoy your next important boondoggle.

I want my port commissioners to travel the world like a lean pack of hungry wolves. I want them to be junket Olympians, capable of handling demanding travel schedules and high-calorie feasts.

I want them to follow Weiss to the Thin Line clinic in Jupiter.

"We don't call ourselves a weight-loss center," explained supervisor Marie Sweetser. "We are a fat-reduction institute."

Now you skeptics out there might be saying, "So why can't our port commissioners try losing weight the old-fashioned way, by eating less?"

Sweetser says dieting isn't in the clinic's plan.

"We don't want people dieting, because then they'll lose precious muscle," she said.

We couldn't have that. We need our port commissioners strong.

We need them to experience the thermogenetic wave therapy that Weiss got.

We need our port commissioners to have cool liquid solution spread on their flabby body parts in 25-minute sessions.

"Whatever part of the body you want to lose weight, that's where it's applied," Sweetser said.

Finally, a smear tactic politicians can get behind.

Or on their behinds.

And so while the magic of thermogenesis lowers the body temperature in the various flabby regions, allowing the metabolism there to speed up and burn fat, the port commissioner can be blissfully reading a travel brochure and pondering the next free trip.

"It's a mobilized treatment," Sweetser said.

For people whose idea of mobile is global.

For port commissioners striving to serve the public with peak performance without having to actually diet or exercise.

Public money must be spent for this worthy cause. It's the least we can do for them.

Let the thermogenetic waves flow. Let the cooling solution melt away their flab.

Let's start with a dab between the ears.

A plea to ease the clogged pipeline of public officials in prison
Oct. 24, 2007

Why wait, your honor?
Free Warren Newell

Judge Kenneth Marra
U.S. District Court, West Palm Beach, FL

Dear Judge Marra:

Thank you for this chance to address the court. I wouldn't be taking up your valuable time as a federal judge if it weren't for the importance of my request.

So, I'll get right to the point.

Please release former Palm Beach County Commissioner Warren Newell from prison.

I know, I know. You haven't sent him to prison yet.

Technically, I suppose, I should wait for your Jan. 11 sentencing of Mr. Newell before I outline the inhumane circumstances of his expected incarceration, and petition for his speedy return to society, where he will (a) care for various older persons, (b) revitalize the area's struggling housing market and (c) make dinner reservations for Valentine's Day.

Did I mention that he suffers from the heartbreak of psoriasis? Or at least, he probably will by mid-January.

These are by no means all of the reasons you should consider Mr. Newell's early release from the prison sentence he hasn't begun to serve, because you were kind enough to delay his sentencing until after the winter holidays.

While the timing of my request may be unorthodox, it is necessary to start the process in what has become an already clogged pipeline of local public officials who are finding prison unpalatable.

As you know, Mr. Newell is the fourth local official who has pleaded guilty to corruption charges, and two of the previously sentenced officials, former West Palm Beach City Commissioners Ray Liberti and Jim Exline, already have filed their early-release requests.

Liberti has been trying to get out of his 18-month prison sentence. And Exline filed his first request, shortly after beginning his 10-month tax evasion sentence.

In fact, Exline was in prison for only 11 days before he began trying to get out. So a Newell pre-incarceration move still falls within a two-week window of Exline's request.

And let me assure you, your honor, Mr. Newell isn't going to come up with something as silly as Exline's restless leg syndrome or his disappointment with the federal prison system's lack of college-level course electives.

I am not privy to all the worthy reasons why you should release Mr. Newell from the prison he isn't in yet, but I can guarantee you that he'll come up with something more compelling.

Did I mention how much Mr. Newell adores Groundhog Day? I mean, they practically called him "Punxsutawney Warren" on the county commission. The saying was, "If you didn't see Newell's shadow on the dais, that meant six more weeks of secret zoning deals."

It would be a crime to have Mr. Newell still behind bars on Feb. 2. But I am a realist, too, your honor. And I realize you have a job to do.

When you sentence him in January, Mr. Newell faces the maximum of a five-year prison sentence for his corruption conviction. And while he may not receive all that time, I realize that he probably will receive some prison time, because it is important that public officials who betray a public trust spend time behind bars to, as the line goes, "send a message to the community."

Whatever that means.

But what is also becoming clear is that our local public officials who are being packed off to prison are sending a message back. And that message is: We want out.

So please, your honor, start thinking about letting Mr. Newell out of the prison sentence he is about to serve.

Did I mention his lifelong dream of marching in a St. Patrick's Day parade?

CHAPTER 13

Divine interventions
What in the name of God is going on here?

Star of Nativity slips earthly bonds despite Wellington's $880 Jesus-protection program

January 2, 2008

What would Jesus say about GPS?

They don't mess around in Wellington.

"You've got a felony-priced baby Jesus," I explained to the village's recreation services director, Paul Schofield.

Schofield said the village had paid $880 for the manger figure, the latest baby Jesus to grace the patch of grass outside the village's eclectic holiday display in front of the community center.

"They're expensive to buy and replace," he said. "It seems that baby Jesus is a popular traveling figure in Wellington."

Last year, two of them disappeared from the Nativity scene, he said. So this season, BJ3 was chained to the crèche and outfitted with a hidden global positioning satellite-tracking device.

Even so, the night after Christmas, the baby Jesus slipped his earthly chains. But this time, the prankster, Danielle Santino, 18, of suburban Lake Worth, was caught, deputies said, with the help of the tracking device.

Deputies said Santino faces a grand-theft charge. Under Florida law, if you steal something that's worth more than $300, you go from misdemeanor petty theft to felony grand theft.

I'm not a lawyer, but I would argue that springing the baby Jesus from the Wellington holiday display is more of an act of mercy than a felony.

It's like a nightmarish Tim Burton movie set out there. Frosty the Snowman. Menorah. Santa. Skeletal reindeer aplenty. Dreidel.

Sheep.

The theme seems to be "Every Piece on Earth" or "O Holy Garage Sale."

Somebody had to liberate the boy from that mess.

And if you're looking to point fingers, how about examining why $880 in public money needs to be spent on a drive-by religious tchotchke?

I'm sure that if Jesus had a say in this, his reputation for mercy and simplicity would lead to his doll being represented at the misdemeanor price level.

Or, better yet, just having the manger outfitted with a sign that said, "Free."

I suspect that people who take baby Jesus statues probably get more out of them, one way or another, than the passing motorists who never even notice.

Wellington has gotten nothing but headaches from its holiday display. The village started out simple, with a Christmas tree and a menorah. Then it added about $5,000 worth of non-religious decorations.

But when a councilman's wife donated a manger scene, the decorations became mired in the contentious mud of church-state debate. The American Civil Liberties Union got interested. Local churches fought back.

Frosty, it was decided, was too large for the manger figures. The village needed a bigger baby Jesus, Mary and Joseph. A local developer stepped in and ponied up $7,000 to super-size the Nativity scene.

And then the Jesuses started vanishing.

I was willing to call it a miracle. But the village went to the chains and the GPS device.

Now that Wellington is in the Jesus-protection program, it's good that the GPS trackers, which were bought to protect generators purchased after recent hurricanes, can safeguard BJ3 for many Christmases to come.

"We'll remove it from Baby Jesus and put it on something else," Schofield said, "and then next year, we'll put it back. We have more than one tracker.

"We might use them on other items, too."

Like Frosty? Please, no. Let somebody take Frosty. No questions asked.

I would think the village would be better off using its GPS trackers for something more important than keeping tabs on its holiday decorations.

For example, I'm sure that The Mall at Wellington Green would be happy to use GPS trackers to alert security about any droopy-pants teenage boys in the area.

'Wooden' you know it? Jesus' face appears, out of the blue, on 20-year-old door
June 9, 2002

Knock, and a miracle will be opened to you? He thinks door has Jesus' eyes; I think knot

I'm not good with miracles. I explain this to the Rev. Thomas Masters, who excels at miracles, and is showing me his latest visitation of the divine upon his humble self.

"It's just a door," I tell him.

We're in his Riviera Beach church, staring at one of the back doors, which miraculously revealed itself last week as the face of Jesus.

A little too miraculously for me.

"Do you see the eyes?" he asks.

"Those are knots in the wood," I say. "Doors have knots. We can go to Home Depot and find the face of Jesus there, too."

I try to explain to him that what looks like eyes to him looks more to me like F-14 Tomcat fighters making their final approach on an aircraft carrier: "See, there's the cockpit. There are the wings."

He's laughing hysterically at me.

"I know. It's ridiculous," I say. "They're not F-14s. They're not eyes, either. They're just knots in the wood. Everything else is just imagination.

"Haven't you ever looked at clouds?"

I'm the perfect foil for Masters.

Every miracle sermon needs the callous nonbeliever. And my

skepticism will be the right touch for his next sermon, when he addresses the faithful at the New Macedonia Missionary Baptist Church.

They're the people who really matter to him.

"What you say is going to have no effect," his assistant-miracle-manager Bennie Herring tells me. "Because they're not going to believe you anyway."

It's really a perfect arrangement. I get to write about Masters' latest shameless attempt at spotlight-grabbing. And he gets to use me as the manifestation of evil, the proof of his saintliness.

The door becomes whatever people want it to become.

The only undisputed miracle would be if Masters wasn't orchestrating this.

He's shepherding his latest production with the skill of a gifted infomercial director, lining up testimonials, turning knots into eyes, eyes into faces, faces into faces of Jesus, and finally, faces of Jesus into proof of Masters' place at the vortex of holiness.

No place for a guy like me. I'm not good with miracles.

Psychologist Steve Alexander is better. He happened to be having breakfast with Masters on political business last week and ended up being on his short list of miracle references.

"God works in ways that requires a modicum of faith to believe," Alexander said. "I can see the eyes. But I can't verify that it's the work of God."

He'll work in a pinch for "outsider verification." But my favorite testimonial comes from Palm Beach County Commissioner Addie Greene, who liked the door so much that she brought her staff back to see it.

"I was afraid to touch it," she said. "I don't know why."

I don't either, Addie. I touched it, and guess what? IT'S JUST WOOD.

I'm sorry for that outburst. I'm just not good with miracles. And besides, this isn't even Masters' best effort. The Jesus in the bathroom window eight years ago was much better. Masters put his hand on the glass and announced that it was going "bump, bump, bump" into his hand.

Moving parts or mysterious secretions. That's the key to top-rate miracles.

The door miracle is pretty low-tech. The old door's been there for more than 20 years. Masters says he spotted the face on it Tuesday night.

Did the door's wood grain re-scramble itself that day, the knots moving to form eyes, the grain shifting to make a nose, a mouth, a beard?

"We're going have to look at videotapes," he says.

I'll save you some time, Rev. The answer is no.

But it doesn't matter. This miracle's got legs. Masters has enough cosmic interpretations to last a few sermons, and that's without going into the church's other back door — which has turned into an angel this week.

Think of it as a back-up miracle.

An angel? It's just a door.

But you don't have to believe me. I'm not good with miracles.

**To ensure brotherly love at holidays,
Delray needs 100-foot Frosty the Pantheistic Snowman**
December 13, 2009

Delray needs Hanukkah spin control

News item: The absence of a Hanukkah menorah near the 100-foot Christmas tree at Old School Square in Delray Beach became a subject of controversy that was averted by the city's last-minute scramble to find a menorah-rental company in time for the start of the eight-day Jewish holiday.

Mayor Woodie McDuffie said the city would revisit its policy on holiday displays.

To: Mayor McDuffie

From: Cerabino Holiday Display Consultants Inc.

Subject: Menorahgate

We here at CHDC have followed with interest the saga of your holiday decoration emergency. And we agree that a comprehensive policy on holiday decorations is both prudent and necessary.

Here are some things we'd like you to consider in the interest of avoiding future "décor-bacles."

By putting a 100-foot fake Christmas tree in the city square, you have literally created a monster decoration. This towering symbol of the Christian holiday casts a shadow on the other decorations.

To correct this problem, choose one of three solutions:

1. Find a 100-foot menorah for next year.

You may have to build one. If so, you can probably get federal stimulus money to do it.

2. Swap the tree for a 100-foot Frosty the Pantheistic Snowman.

This Frosty has exchanged his stovepipe hat for a yarmulke, and the mechanism at his base allows the giant snowman to swivel toward Mecca once a day. For extra points: Frosty could sport a scarf in Kwanzaa colors.

3. Display a real Christmas tree.

Holiday music is a particularly thorny problem. There are way too many Christmas songs and, as far as we can tell, only one widely known Hanukkah song.

Dreidel, Dreidel, Dreidel also has the misfortune of being so annoying and repetitive that the human ear can stand only about 30 seconds of it at a time.

Consider this solution:

Play only Christmas songs written by Jewish composers.

These would include *Rudolph the Red-Nosed Reindeer, Silver Bells, Let It Snow* and perhaps the greatest Christmas song of all, *White Christmas*, which was written by Irving Berlin.

After every fifth Christmas song, play *Dreidel, Dreidel, Dreidel* for 30 seconds — or until somebody screams.

As a side note: Wiccans have music, too. But we don't recommend you start playing it, because it will just create confusion that there's a yoga class in progress.

We recommend that you establish a Holiday Decoration Response Team to deal with these fast-moving man-made public relations disasters. Just keep in mind that whatever you do, it will offend someone. There are no right answers here, only a selection of perilous, imperfect choices.

Good luck, and please, do us a favor by destroying this memo to spare us some apologizing.

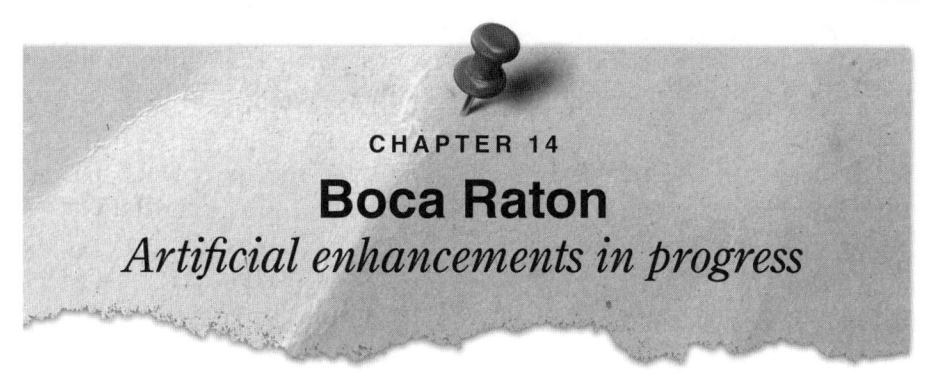

CHAPTER 14
Boca Raton
Artificial enhancements in progress

**What's in a name? Plenty.
The art of raising money is alive and well at Boca museum**
February 2, 2001

Name-dropping hits new high at Boca museum

I just went to the new Boca Raton Museum of Art.

The museum moved last week into its spacious two-story digs on the north end of Mizner Park, and I read about the Picasso exhibit there. But I had a tough time keeping my eyes on the art, because it was far more fascinating to peruse the oversize donor plaques that covered the walls.

The art of raising money, it seems, is the $13.3 million museum's permanent and most visible exhibit.

In case you're thinking of giving money to the museum, you'd better hurry, because there isn't much left that hasn't been titled to donors, whose names have been memorialized in bold, black lettering on big rectangles of thick glass bolted to the nearest wall.

In fact, even the walls are named.

When you walk up to the museum, you'll notice the Benjamin and Sarah Torchinsky pool, which leads you to the Gary and Loretta Rabiner portico. You walk through the glass doors (naming rights still available!) and into the Mary Ann and Harold E. Perper reception lobby.

Don't go straight, or you'll walk into the Babs and Maury Young wall. Hang a left, and you'll be in the Leonard and Phyllis Greenberg gift shop.

A right turn will take you into the main gallery, and the Wall of

Honor — a kind of Vietnam Memorial of tax write-offs. Keep walking down the Dani and Jack Sonnenblick promenade and you'll come to a crossroads.

Do you go left and take the Phyllis and Jerry Rubin elevator to the second floor? Or do you go right, and walk up the Charlotte and Norman F. Cado grand staircase?

I weighed my options while taking a sip from the Dr. Herbert and Mrs. Lenore Wachtel drinking fountains.

Apparently, the Wachtels got naming rights to both water fountains on the first floor. Upstairs, the two drinking fountains got divided between donors. Morton and Joanne Kornreich got the kiddie fountain, and Herman and Millicent Eisenberg got the taller fountain.

But let's get back to the first floor, where the Picasso exhibit was. Not that I spent much time with his work. My eyes kept falling on sponsorship signs for trellis columns, parking spaces, a security vault, and even the Tamara Tennant Interior Design loading dock.

I was wondering what sort of jack it would take to get a loading dock named after you. So I called the Boca Raton interior designer.

"Did you always want to get a loading dock named after you?" I asked Tamara Tennant.

"It kind of came down to that there really wasn't a whole lot left," Tennant said. "And I just thought the loading dock would be a hoot."

Tennant said she could have opted for a bench, or combined her money with some other donors to get something with more panache. But for $10,000, getting sole naming rights to a loading dock seemed to be the best option.

"I thought it was especially funny when I went to the grand opening to see that they put our plaque for the loading dock on the first floor of the gallery," she said.

(It's near the Edwin and Ethyl Blatt palm-tree plaque.)

And yes, in case you're wondering, the bathrooms weren't spared, either. I didn't check the women's restrooms, but the second-floor men's room has been spoken for by the Sonnenblicks. The restroom, and its various appliances, comes as a package deal.

Things really get divvied up in the sculpture garden, where the Gloria and David Furman wall is illuminated by the Charlotte and Morris Robinson lights, which sit in the Rhonda and Emanuel Shemin garden.

Boca Raton: Artificial enhancements in progress

If it's all too much for you, you can make a hasty exit from an unpainted wooden shadowbox gate.

Of course it is. It's the Janice and Stuart Flaum gate.

Millions in charity donations at risk after profile of Boca benefactor reveals 'warts and all'
March 1, 1992

Charities grovel, but countess says heads must roll

The Countess speaks.

"I want these two people out," she says. "The editor and the writer. They don't belong in Boca Raton."

Wayne Ezell. Sharon Geltner. Banished from the pink-flamingo kingdom to some journalistic Elba? For what crime?

Printing the truth.

Last week, Geltner wrote a story in the *The News* of Boca Raton, pointing out in great detail how The Countess Henrietta de Hoernle, 79, isn't a real countess.

She and her husband, Adolph, who got rich from a Yonkers, N.Y., tool-and-die company, bought their Knights of Malta titles and gold crosses for $20,000 from a huckster, the story said.

It went on to report how the couple also changed their name — going from the pedestrian "horn-el" pronunciation to the snazzier "horn-lee" and then wedging the "de" in there for that extra regal touch.

Shocking journalism? Hardly.

At most, it made The Countess look a little common.

"The story is a profile," Geltner explained, "and profiles are supposed to get up close and personal. It's supposed to show warts and all.

"It's the longest project I ever had. It was months in the making. I had to research the arcane field of knighthood. Every word of it is true."

Ah, now we're back to the crime.

Printing the truth can get newspapers in trouble. In Colombia, a newspaper earns its spurs by printing wide-eyed stories about the drug cartel.

In Boca, *The News* is finding out that it has stepped out on that same journalistic ledge by printing a wide-eyed story about a sacred cow on the city's social/charity scene.

The Countess is one of the deepest pockets in town. She has given millions to local charities. And her will, she says, had been written to give some $22 million to a dozen local charities.

So when *The News* poked a hole in her royal claim, it might have seemed harmless at first. But to all the organizations in town that depend on Countess cash, the story was trouble.

They don't care if it's accurate — not if it's going to upset their benefactor.

Alan Kauffman, a Cystic Fibrosis Foundation fund-raiser and her attorney, told the newspaper: "In essence, you've kicked Santa Claus in the teeth."

The story may have made The Countess look a little silly, but not half as silly as the hubbub it raised.

The Countess responded these past few days by rewriting her will, taking all the Boca charities out of it, all $22 million worth.

"It's signed, sealed and delivered," she said. "If they condone what the paper wrote, then that will be it."

The message to the charities is clear. Make the paper eat the story, or get ready for a royal goose egg from The Countess.

"They'll be affected," she said of the charities. "If they take this lying down, then it's up to them."

The paper's editor, Ezell; and the reporter, Geltner; must be fired, and *The News* must print an apology, she said. Then she'll put the Boca charities back in her will.

How about just an apology?

"That's not enough," she said. "My mind will change when those two people are gone."

Of course, there's nothing in the story to retract.

"I really deeply regret if The Countess has been hurt by this," editor Ezell said. "But we've printed a story, and the veracity of it has not been questioned."

Veracity? What's veracity got to do with it?

It's about money. The charities are in such a dither over The Countess' threat that they've flooded the newspaper with angry letters and have planned to take out pro-Countess ads in newspapers this week.

"The ad won't be an attack," Kauffman said, "but one that says how grateful we are of the Count and Countess."

Meanwhile, Sally Stewart, a board member of the Humanitarian Society and the owner of Boca Laser, has made and handed out more than a hundred "I ♥ Countess de Hoernle" buttons.

Letters. Ads. Buttons.

Stand by for some heavy groveling.

And at *The News*, it's time to send the lookouts up to the pink parapets and to restock the moat with alligators.

The Countess is giving orders. And the society cartel is on the march.

Country Network's immigrants – er, employees – have to learn to appreciate Boca's vittles, customs, lingo
Friday, July 15, 2011

Country fans, South is just state of mind

Dear country-music employee:

I'd like to be the first to welcome you to your new home in Boca Raton.

Like many people here, I was surprised when I learned that The Country Network, a TV channel that broadcasts country-music videos 24 hours a day, is moving its headquarters from Music Row in Nashville to Yamato Road in Boca Raton.

Good-bye, Grand Ole Opry; hello, ornery ole grandma.

The thought of Boca becoming a focal point of country music was, well, only slightly more plausible than the city becoming the new headquarters for a mountain-climbing channel.

Don't get me wrong. We're thrilled that you're coming. The Business Development Board of Palm Beach County is downright giddy over your move, pointing out that it may bring 20 new jobs to the area, not to mention a boatload of big hats.

We need all the new jobs we can get, and we plan to do everything in our power to make you feel comfortable here in this new, somewhat foreign land you've chosen to call home.

Let's just get something out of the way, right off the bat. Boca Raton, despite its latitude, is not really part of the South. It just looks that way on the map.

So, you're going to have to transition from "hee haw" to "oy vey" as you learn the new language.

When you say "Howdy" in Tennessee, it means "Hello." But in Boca, it's just the first part of a question, as in, "Howdy afford to take another trip to Long Island, Gina?"

You'll learn to love the local people here. Eventually. Probably not at first. And maybe never, if you shop at the Costco on Saturday afternoons.

In anticipation of your arrival, we'll try to devise some gestures to make you feel welcome.

For example, maybe we can convert a small section of Dixie Highway to dirt road and get Tri-Rail to run more southbound trains, the preferred direction for trains in county-music lyrics.

As for all the city's sushi restaurants, it wouldn't kill them if they stuck a "bait" sign in the window.

The hunting, unfortunately, will be problematic, and limited mostly to bargains at the Town Center mall, although we do have some of the best rabid otter this side of the Hillsboro Canal.

Even so, you'll notice very few gun racks in the vehicles around here. The only racks in Boca are the ones engineered by plastic surgeons.

But who knows? Once your country-music station takes root here, it might inspire a whole new generation of Boca-country songs.

And the next crop of country stars may soon be hanging around the Flakowitz Bagel Inn with nothing but a dream, a guitar — and a poppy-seed bagel, toasted, with a shmear.

It could lead to such new Boca-country hits as *Mommas, Don't Let Your Babies Grow Up to Shop With Chihuahuas, Data Miner's Daughter, Your Cheatin' Accountant, I Walk to Powerline,* and *I'm So Over-Leveraged, I Could Cry.*

This could be the start of something special.

At last: Boca's oppressed Italian-Americans have a spokesman, even if he isn't one of them
October 13, 1994

How a white guy from Boca leads offended minority

In case you haven't noticed, we Italian-Americans in Palm Beach County have a new leader.

I'm thrilled about this. We've always lacked somebody to make us feel like a true oppressed minority.

It's a rare calling, to be able to persuade people like me — white, male, heterosexual — that I might actually qualify as being slighted in some way.

I've always thought I was part of the problem.

But now, there's hope.

Yes, I too can feel cheated by history. I too can feel outraged by the insensitive rule of the majority. I too can feel drowned by mainstream America.

That's because we Italian-Americans have a new leader, a man who is making the voice of the oppressed ring out in the ghetto that is Boca Raton.

His name is Alvin Adams.

I know, the name doesn't sound too Italian to me, either.

You'd think we could find a Vinny somewhere, or at least somebody with a vowel at the end of his last name, instead of a guy who sounds like he just stepped off the Mayflower.

But we Italians can't be too choosy.

We have to take our leaders where we find them. We've been minding our own business for so long that we haven't had the time to develop a resource pool of troublemakers to choose from.

So we end up with a guy named Alvin as our head goombah.

He runs the Sicilian-American Social Club of Florida, based in Boca Raton.

Alvin got on the map by sticking up for Christopher Columbus.

The city of Boca Raton had planned to scrap the Columbus Day holiday this year to placate black residents and workers who were complaining that the city didn't shut down for Martin Luther King Day.

So the city council members did something they thought was harmless: swap Columbus for King.

But they didn't count on Alvin, who suddenly emerged as the voice of indignation, a veritable civil rights leader in a group you'd expect would be content to just organize bocce tournaments.

Naturally, the city caved in, shutting down on Columbus Day.

Then, Alvin and about 100 others in his group packed the city council chambers to persuade the city to shut down for Columbus Day every year.

Naturally, the city caved in.

Nobody wants to go against a leader of the oppressed — even if he happens to be a white guy from Boca.

And so we Italian-Americans have a right to be proud.

I know I was especially proud on Columbus Day when I went to put my garbage on the curb and realized that I would have the pleasure of keeping it for an extra day.

Yes, the guys who pick up my garbage (three black guys) had the day off.

No doubt they were partaking in a group discussion on 15th-century celestial navigation, while I was overflowing with Italian-American pride and Hefty bags.

I tried to figure out the logic of that. But then I realized that I probably couldn't because I wasn't looking at this the right way.

I had to start thinking like an oppressed person, I kept telling myself.

And forcing other people to take a day off to honor the standard-bearer for my ethnic group is what being oppressed is all about.

Or as my leader, Alvin, told the city council that night: "I hope you enjoyed your day off."

Take that, you straight-out-of-the-jar, sauce-eating politicians. That'll teach you to mess with us.

Go ahead. Make my day off.

So, yes. I feel great that my taxes will help pay for the $35,000 in overtime pay for city workers that the new Columbus Day holiday has created.

Good deeds in our midst: People you'd be lucky to meet

That's the least I can do to ensure that all you white-bread-eating people out there start treating us Italian-Americans like a touchy, quick-to-offend ethnic group.

Because that's what respect is all about these days: the fear of offending.

And as my head goombah, Alvin "Big Holiday" Adams has taught me, you can't be too white, too male or too Boca to be an offended minority.

Alvin's even going to organize a parade for us next year. I can't wait.

If we're smart, we'll figure out a way to invite a few of the city garbage trucks.

This way, we can bring our garbage so we don't have leave it roasting in the sun for another day in honor of Columbus.

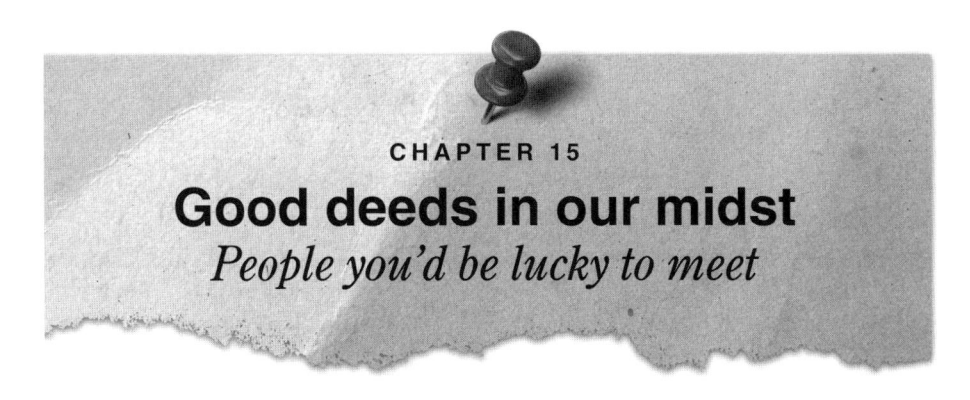

CHAPTER 15

Good deeds in our midst
People you'd be lucky to meet

The unexpected booty was pricey, but the happy ending was priceless
November 18, 1998

Story has nice ring to it: Love, loss prompt good deed

It wasn't until the day after Halloween that the girl dumped her haul of trick-or-treat candy from the pillowcase.

And there it was, among all the candy bars — an engagement ring, a gold band with a solitaire diamond setting. Yahaira Oms, 9, was at her grandma's house that day. When she found the ring, she called her mom in Lantana.

"I told her it was probably something fake," said the mom, Maria Ocasio.

But the girl knew better.

"I looked on the inside, and it said '14 karat,'" she said.

The grandma said she should keep the ring. It would be worth a lot of money.

But the little girl thought of her dog, Blackie, who ran away and disappeared when she was 7. And she connected losing Blackie to the woman who was missing this ring.

"I thought she must feel the same way I felt with Blackie," the girl said.

The girl's mother, divorced for seven years, raising two kids alone and working two jobs to do it, could have thought about pawning the ring for cash, money she certainly could use.

But she thought about "the good old days when I was in love."

So the mother and daughter, arriving at the decision from different directions, had known that somehow they must find the woman whose ring had slipped into the bulging pillowcase of candy.

This story may sound familiar. I wrote about it a few days ago, but from the perspective of the woman who had lost the ring.

Laura Beaupre, 27, of suburban West Palm Beach, had no idea who the people were who found her ring. All she knew was that, after two days of fruitless searching, tears and regret, she had given up hope of ever getting back her engagement ring.

And then suddenly, a woman and her daughter showed up at her door with the ring, handed it to her and drove away.

Beaupre was too tearful to even get the names of the mom and daughter, and they refused the reward money she had tried to give them. Weeks later, she still felt a lingering need to thank them. So she told me her story as a way of reaching them.

"Maybe if they read it," Beaupre said, "they'll realize how happy they made me."

A co-worker of the Lantana mom then called me, telling me the identity of the mother and daughter.

I talked to Ocasio while she was working her day job, as a secretary at John I. Leonard High School in Greenacres.

"Did you ever think about keeping the ring and selling it?" I asked.

Good deeds in our midst: People you'd be lucky to meet

"No," she said.

She couldn't do that to a woman who, unlike her, still had a reason to want to wear her engagement ring. And there was something else.

"I hear so many things about single parents," Ocasio said, "that because of divorced parents, kids grow up screwed up."

"I don't want my kids growing up like that," she said. "I want them to be self-sufficient. I want to show them they can make it on their own."

Ocasio, 33, who moved here from Puerto Rico 14 years ago, wants to become a teacher some day. To make that happen, in addition to her two jobs, she goes to class one night a week at Florida Atlantic University in Boca Raton.

Two nights after Halloween, Ocasio and her daughter drove to the neighborhood where her fourth-grade daughter had trick-or-treated. It didn't take long to find the "lost ring" signs and the tearful Beaupre.

"I felt embarrassed," Ocasio said. "She was crying, and taking out her checkbook, and I said, 'No, I'd better just go.'"

Ocasio's daughter still thinks of that night she gave back the ring.

"It made me feel really good to make a person happy," Yahaira said.

Laura Beaupre was lucky, lucky that her ring had fallen into the hands of two people who knew about loss — whether of man or beast — and knew that the happiest ending of all was priceless.

Worker's flu + nice boss + flat tire = lucky break for injured feline
August 31, 2001

Daring cat rescue in I-95 traffic was destined to be, laborer says

Kerry Modder is not a religious man. But the cat that seems to melt in his big hands is a strange addition to his life, one that he finds difficult to explain in worldly terms.

They're an odd couple, the dainty young cat and this big laborer — a scruffy 50-year-old floor installer with a pickup truck and a big old soft spot that you might not imagine at first.

"I just couldn't turn my back on her," he said about the cat he calls Xena, Warrior Princess.

Modder found the cat on Interstate 95 earlier this summer. He was driving from his West Palm Beach apartment to Fort Pierce to install linoleum tile in a school cafeteria.

The week before, he had been two days shy of completing the job when he came down with the flu, combined with a double dose of pink eye.

"I missed an entire week of work," he said. "Not good."

But at least the contractor didn't give the job away. After Modder got well, he drove to Fort Pierce with his friend and co-worker Rick Bragg to try to finish the overdue job.

But then came a series of events that Modder would also describe as "not good."

First, there was the flat tire on the highway near the Gatlin Boulevard exit. Then he discovered his spare was flat. Then Bragg's cell-phone was out of its service area. They were on the side of the highway for more than an hour.

"I was standing at the passenger side of my truck at the time, and I asked my friend for my smokes," Modder said. "As soon as he handed them to me, I turned around, looking to the rear of my truck, when I see an animal in the middle of the slow lane of I-95."

The cat must have been thrown or dropped from a passing car. Cars were zooming over and around it, and the animal was bleeding, trying to make it to the side of the road, but unable to get onto its feet.

Modder ran into the highway.

"I've known Kerry for a long time," Bragg said. "But I saw a part of him that day that I hadn't seen before. He was out there in the road, and a car missed him by about 3 inches."

He got back to the truck, holding the cat, which was bleeding from the mouth and from one of her eyes. Two of her legs appeared to be broken, and she was hyperventilating from the early stages of shock.

Modder had a decision to make: to drop the cat and go on to his job, or to miss another day's work and take on this hardship case.

"This is where the spiritual thing comes in," Modder explained. "We deduced that I was supposed to be sick the week before. If not, we would have already finished the job. The contractor was supposed to be the easygoing fellow that he is, or he would have called to get someone else to finish his job.

"I was supposed to have that flat tire along with a bad spare. If the spare was OK, I would have been on my way in only 10 minutes or so."

The cat, they said, was fate.

"We both had goose-pimples all the way back to West Palm," Modder said.

Without charge, the Animal Rescue League of the Palm Beaches repaired the animal's broken palate, the source of bleeding from its mouth. But the cat needed surgery for its broken bones, something a private veterinarian would have to do.

Modder walked into the office of Jay Butan, a Lake Worth veterinarian. A friend had told Modder that the vet's office was full of cats he refused to euthanize. And this vet wouldn't ask about money first.

"He took her right out of my hands," Modder said. "I had blood all over me."

Butan said there was something about Modder that resonated with him.

"You could see that this little cat meant something to him," the vet said. "He had that look in his face that said I needed to take care of his cat."

The cat was flea-infested and anemic from intestinal worms. It needed a blood transfusion and surgery on its right rear leg, a surgery that it wouldn't be strong enough to endure.

So the vet kept the cat for more than a month, fattening it up and making it strong enough to survive the eventual amputation of its leg.

The bill, even at a discounted $1,128 total, was more than Modder could afford.

"I live week to week," he explained.

He applied for credit and was turned down.

"It's not that I have bad credit," he said. "I have no credit. I pay cash for everything."

So Modder and the vet made a deal: He'd pay $40 a week.

Modder's friends want to help out. They're organizing a money-raising event next month at the El Cid Bar in West Palm Beach.

154   Writing Like a Taller Person: The Best of Frank Cerabino

Meanwhile, Xena the three-legged cat likes to stay among the pots and pans in his kitchen, away from the only other resident of Modder's apartment: a diabetic 18-year-old cat named Ashes.

"Ashes is getting old," said Modder's friend Bragg. "And Kerry is needing a new friend. Everything happens for a reason. I tell Kerry, though, that if he's going to spend so much money on a new cat, at least he should get one with all four legs."

Butan said he's not too concerned whether or not Modder will ever pay the bill for Xena.

"Whatever he does, he does," Butan said.

"I'm not very religious," the vet said. "But every once in a while, God smacks you in the head and tells you to do something."

Taunters carrying World Series tickets can't dampen spirits of their target: Happy dad
October 19, 1997

A dad's determination gets son once-in-a-lifetime ticket

As the fans began flowing into Gate H outside Pro Player Stadium, Jay Harris, an unshaven, potbellied, out-of-work flower-truck driver, stood patiently next to his 13-year-old son, Jimmy.

Harris and his son had been in that spot for an hour, standing like mute sentries behind a piece of white board that said it all: "I need 1 FREE ticket for my son."

The father had scribbled the message on the board, underlining the word "son."

Then as an afterthought, he had written on the sign, "I'll wait outside for him."

It was a pretty silly idea, even Harris had to admit. All around them, people were negotiating the prices on upper-deck seats for more than a hundred dollars apiece, and there he was, asking for a free one.

But it was the only shot he had of getting his kid into a World Series game. So after Jimmy's youth-league football game Saturday afternoon in Hollywood, the father and his son took the drive to Pro

Good deeds in our midst: People you'd be lucky to meet

Player Stadium, spent the $5 for parking and waited. And waited.

"If somebody will take him in, I'll just wait in the parking lot until the game's over," the father explained.

No, he said, he didn't care for a ticket for himself. Just his kid.

Most people avoided eye contact with the Harrises and their pathetic sign.

Some smiled. They all moved on, except for the scalpers who figured Harris' sign was a clever way to begin bargaining for a ticket.

"No," Harris said. "If I could afford a ticket, I would buy one. I need a free one."

Then somebody stopped. Christina Fernandez, 41, of Miami had two boys — and something bothering her.

"It wasn't until I was driving to the stadium when I realized I had an extra ticket. I had four tickets, and there were only three of us."

Fernandez was taking her old college roommate's children to the game.

Devin, 10, and Michael, 13, had flown from New Orleans just to go to the game.

"When we got to the stadium, there were all these people looking to buy tickets," she said. "But I just didn't think it was right to sell it to just anyone, and then I saw this man standing out there with his son."

Jimmy Harris was wearing a Marlins Tasmanian Devil T-shirt and a Marlins cap, and he was carrying a thermos of water, an egg-salad sandwich and a vanilla pudding.

"He looked about the same age as the boys," the woman said. "And I figured this would be perfect. Nothing's better than a kid."

Jay Harris and Christina Fernandez spoke only briefly to each other before Harris' son disappeared with the strange woman through the turnstiles.

"I could tell she was a good woman," Harris said.

Harris didn't know exactly where his son would be — somewhere in Section 448 – and after the game he'd be waiting for him outside the same gate.

"Today's your lucky day," Fernandez told the boy, as they sat in their ninth-row upper-deck seats right behind home plate — the best upper-deck seats in the stadium.

It was still more than two hours before game time. Harris, just for kicks, flipped his sign over and wrote another message: "I need 1 FREE ticket."

No cute kid standing next to him this time. Just another guy looking to get into the game.

Eddie Gonzalez, another man looking for a ticket, came up to Harris and told him it was hopeless.

"If somebody gives you a ticket, I'll trade it for this," Gonzalez said, showing Harris his wristwatch. "Nobody's going to give you a ticket. I've been trying to buy one for $100, and the lowest I've been offered is $125."

A few feet away, John Puckett, 35, of North Lauderdale was offering to buy any ticket for $80, but wasn't getting any takers.

Without the boy standing next to him, Jay Harris was getting a lot of taunts and jeers from fans walking into the game with tickets.

"What's he on?" one guy remarked to his friend.

Others waved their tickets in front of his face.

Harris just smiled.

"They don't know," he said. "They laugh because they don't think it would ever happen. They don't know that there are people out there like that woman."

At about 7:30, Harris put away his sign. His wife, Janet, a manicurist, was waiting at home to watch the game on television. She was surprised when she found out that her husband's plan had actually worked.

"But I guess I shouldn't be," she said. "He's pretty determined."

But he won't be trying it again.

"No," said Harris. "This is something you only do once."

By game time, the outside of Pro Player Stadium was ringed with unhappy fans who had failed to get a last-minute ticket to the game. Harris sat among them, watching the game from a TV screen inside a parking-lot beer tent.

But he wasn't unhappy. Because, somewhere in the roar of that thundering stadium crowd, was his boy.

And on this night, that was way more than enough.

Big-hearted firefighter comes to the rescue of woman who lost her 'drive'

August 9, 1998

His priceless gift rescues a damsel in auto distress

Stan Cooper figured it was some kind of scam. Had to be.

Never saw anything like it before. And Cooper has been in the car-repair business for 32 years; enough time, he figured, to have seen it all. The man standing in Cooper's North American Transmissions shop in West Palm Beach told him his story.

His name is Ron Bond, a 36-year-old Boca Raton firefighter who lives in Lake Worth. He was on his way home, about 8:30 a.m. last week, when he pulled off Interstate 95 onto the northbound ramp at Sixth Avenue South.

While stopping for the light there, he noticed that the car in front of him wasn't moving. It was a 1991 Buick Skylark with 136,000 miles on it and a teary-eyed middle-aged Dominican woman in it.

She couldn't get it moving. And she couldn't speak much English, either.

Bond pushed the woman's car to the side of the road and gave her a ride home.

Elida Martinez had been on her way to interview for an office-cleaning job when her Skylark gave out. Martinez lives with her English-speaking daughter, Jacqueline, 17, who is supporting both of them with a job in the photo lab at an Eckerd drugstore.

"They were not non-working lazy people," Bond said. "The house was immaculate. I can imagine jobs are hard to find, especially if your language is bad."

Bond asked Martinez what she planned to do about the car. She said she couldn't afford to send it to a shop. Maybe a friend would be able to fix it.

Bond got his tools and drove back out to the car with the women to see if he could fix it. Something was wrong with the transmission.

Instead of driving them back home and wishing them luck, he drove along Military Trail and stopped at one transmission place. But nobody helped him right away.

"A voice told me to go to another place," Bond said.

So he drove up the road and found Cooper's shop. First time there.

Cooper listened to Bond, looked at the women and tried to figure out the scam.

"He wanted me to send a tow truck to pick up the car and fix it," Cooper said. "Then he gave me his phone number and said, 'Call me when it's done. I'll be paying you.'"

Cooper picked up the Buick and called Bond with the bad news: a $1,200 transmission overhaul.

OK, Bond said. Do it.

When the car was done, Cooper called Bond, who walked in the shop — this time, without Martinez and her daughter.

"I'm thinking he's going to write me a bad check now," Cooper said.

But instead, Bond pulled out cash.

"I kept looking over his shoulder," Cooper said, "and he asked me, 'What are you looking at?' and I said, 'I'm looking for your white horse.'"

Cooper, who was so bowled over by the man's generosity that he knocked a few hundred dollars off the price of the repair, told me the story the next day.

"Every time I think about it, I get a big smile," Cooper said. "I mean, I can see a wealthy guy doing something like this, but this guy was just a regular working man."

I called Bond.

"Why?" I asked.

"It may sound funny, but if you believe in God like I do, I just knew that I had to do something," Bond said. "I had no idea how much money it would end up being, but I knew I had to do it. Somebody else was looking out for that lady and her family that day, and I just got to be part of it."

Are you going to see them again?

"I don't have a reason to go back," he said. "I gave them a chance to say thank you, but that's it."

I talked to Martinez's daughter.

"It's not every day a stranger pays for a $900 repair on your car," I said.

"Are you serious? That much!" she said. "Nine-hundred dollars!"
"You didn't know?" I asked.
"No," she said. "He didn't want us to know how much it cost."

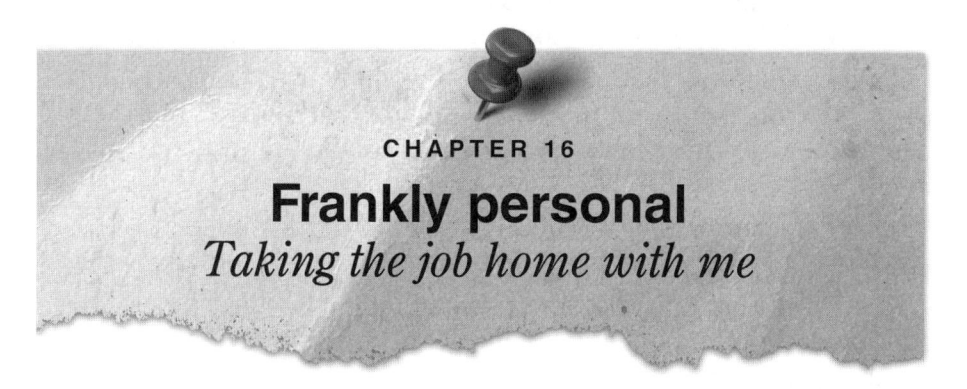

CHAPTER 16
Frankly personal
Taking the job home with me

Frank becomes frozen in time as a Beverly Hillbilly of Boca Raton
June 13, 2008

Google's new street views disservice to community

Dear Google:

I am writing to ask you to reconsider this "street view" mapping service you have inflicted on our community. At first, I thought it was nifty that you recently added Palm Beach County to your street-level image service.

I've read about your technology, how you've sent a Volkswagen equipped with a $45,000, roof-mounted 11-lens camera system to ride up and down streets, capturing images of homes and businesses at 30 frames per second.

And then how you turned these photos into an interactive visual tour, allowing anybody with a computer to Google an address, then use the keyboard mouse to move around the block with 360-degree views from the road.

So naturally, I Googled my home in Boca Raton and clicked on the "street view" tab, expecting to see a rather generic view of my home.

But what I saw, instead, was my wife in her nightgown.

Our home was somewhere in the background. But I was mesmerized by the scene in the driveway area, where my wife, wearing what we call her "Tijuana dress," stood talking to the driver of a large white vehicle parked in our driveway.

I showed your photo to my wife, and she claims it was her boss, although for the record, her boss drives a different make and model of vehicle. (I'll let you know how this shakes out in a future letter.)

But it's safe to say that had my wife known that you were rolling down the block with your all-seeing camera that Monday morning, I doubt she would have been standing there in her TJ muumuu talking to her boss. Allegedly.

And yes, I know it was a Monday morning. That would explain the trash bags and recycling bins piled on my swale.

This has brought up another problem. I don't like leaving empty garbage cans sitting outside my house all day Monday until I retrieve them after getting home from work.

So I take the kitchen trash bags out of the garbage cans and pile them on the swale on pickup mornings.

My wife says these piles of garbage bags look shabby and that I should just leave them in the can. But I have always said, "Who cares how it looks? It's not like they're going to be there long."

I bring the bags out at 7 a.m., and usually the truck picks them up by 10.

So thank you, Google, for driving by sometime during those three unsightly hours.

Oh, and another thing, my son doesn't have that junky pickup truck anymore.

It's the other thing in the foreground in some of the views of my home. My son sold that clunker for $500 and now has a much more reputable-looking vehicle parked outside our home.

In other home improvement news, since you drove by, we've planted begonias in the barren spots in the flower beds and replaced some of the dead patches on the lawn.

If only we knew you were coming.

So here's my solution.

You need to send your Big Brother-mobile back to my block and retake the views of my house.

I am a borderline upstanding member of this community who can't afford to have my domestic situation memorialized in such a sketchy way. My Google image has been tarnished.

Frankly personal: Taking the job home with me

The way things look now — piles of garbage, beat-up pickup truck, wife socializing in the driveway in her nightgown — I'm frozen in time as a kind of Beverly Hillbilly of Boca Raton.

If you give me notice, the next time you drive by I'll make sure my son washes his new car, my wife is dressed and the garbage is in the can.

College tour provides test of Frank's parenting skills (and skivvies)
April 13, 2005

Father and son shed more than inhibitions

If you have teenagers, you're constantly thinking about being a good influence on them.

You know the day is drawing near when they'll be on their own, either in college or the work world, and by then it's too late. You'll only be able to hope they have enough sense to make responsible decisions. I mention this as an introduction to a recent trip I took with my teenage son. We were visiting a college campus in Florida.

We arrived early, and had an hour to kill before our appointment in the admissions office. So we wandered around campus, winding our way toward the cafeteria.

That's when we first saw the group of about a dozen male and female students clustered on a second-floor balcony of a nearby dorm.

It was about 3 in the afternoon, and apparently well into happy hour. There was a celebration going on because one of them had passed a big exam that day, and to commemorate the achievement, everyone who happened to walk by the dorm was told the same thing:

"Take off your pants!" the chorus of voices implored.

We watched the scene from a safe distance as a female student who happened to be walking by simply stopped, put down her books, and stepped out of her jeans. She then carried them with her books, and continued on in her underwear to cheers from the balcony.

"Let's go another way," I suggested to my son.

We were going to the gym, which would have taken us in front of that dorm.

But we figured out another route that took us safely away from the balcony brigade, which could be heard bellowing, "Take off your pants!" followed by cheering, as each new pedestrian approached, and presumably, complied.

After the gym, we started making our way back through campus and ended up following a path that took us to the dorm from the other direction. As soon as we rounded the corner, we were spotted by the balcony celebrants, who sized us up instantly.

"Prospective student and his father, take off your pants! Take off your pants! Take off your pants!"

This was not a parenting situation I had ever come close to imagining. This wasn't like a judgment call about driving to Jupiter, or sanctioning a weekend sleep-over. This was new ground, and a decision was needed quickly.

We could either turn on our heels and flee, keep walking and pretend not to hear them, or do the unthinkable.

The student who just passed her test was imploring us not to violate an alleged tradition, one that I suspected had only begun between the second and third beers.

We kept walking, getting closer and closer.

"You wearing boxers?" I asked my son.

He nodded. Well, it would be no big deal for him. I was the guy in the tighty-whities.

"What do you think?" I asked, but I was already undoing my belt.

We paused there for a moment, father and son, both with our pants around our ankles, receiving a kind of college acceptance that doesn't come via the postal service.

After being fully clothed again and heading toward the admissions office, I tried to summarize the event in a rational, fatherly way.

"Sometimes," I said, "you just gotta . . . It seemed at the time . . ."

But there was no use. My son was still erupting in erratic bursts of laughter.

A few minutes later, we were in the admissions office, where a group of other parents and prospective students had gathered to begin a campus tour.

"Would you like to go on a tour?" an admissions counselor asked us.

"No," I said. "We've already been."

Frankly personal: Taking the job home with me

On Take Your Daughter to Work Day, guess who gets worked over?
April 28, 1995

Nothing tops a daughter's day like Jell-O

It's Thursday, and I have a formidable case of writer's block. A 40-pound case. My daughter, Natalie.

She's 5 years old, going on 14. "Write about Oklahoma," she says, as she sits next to me and looks at my blank computer screen.

"What would I say?"

"The bombing. The bad people," she tells me. "They should be in the electric chair."

Somehow, I don't think she's going to end up being a humor columnist.

But I wanted to take her to work with me as part of the national Take Our Daughters to Work Day. I'd been looking forward to it.

One of the most vivid memories I have is the day many years ago my father took me to work with him. He drove a sales route for Entenmann's Bakery, and I can still see us both barreling down the Long Island Expressway, eating peach pies right out of the boxes as the wind and passing traffic roared through the truck's open door.

No way I could match that.

"Will we go to meetings?" Natalie asks me.

How pathetic. To think that the most exciting thing your father does is go to meetings.

"No," I say.

I want to tell her something . . . something more exciting than that. But all I could come up with is, "We'll go to lunch."

As we drive toward the office, she starts with the questions.

"Who's your boss?"

"Fred."

"Will he be my boss today?"

"Well . . . yeah, I guess."

She looks perplexed.

"Unless," I quickly add, "you want me to be your boss."

"Yeah, I want you."

This is going to work out just fine.

I have three column ideas. Certainly, I could wrestle one of them into this space. But I can't seem to get very far.

"Daddy?"

"Yes."

"My friends say the hair on my arms is ugly."

"It's not ugly," I said. "It's beautiful. It's peach fuzz."

"Mommy shaves her arms and legs," Natalie answers.

"Well, that's different . . .

"She says if I shave my hair it will look like yours," Natalie says, pointing to my hairy wrist.

"You wouldn't want that, would you?" I say.

"No," she says, clearly repulsed.

I call home.

"She said I shave my arms?" my wife says.

"Yes."

"I don't. Where did she get that from? What else is she telling you?" my wife asks.

"She wants to start shaving."

This must be what psychologists mean when they talk about the importance of having quality time with your children. You find out that your 5-year-old thinks about lathering up her forearms.

Natalie sits next to me, pecking away at the keys of another computer terminal. She gets her "column" done in record time, pausing in her random pecks only long enough to ask me how to spell "Oklahoma." She needs something else to do.

"OK, when the phone rings, you can answer it."

I rationalize that my behavior could only be considered sexist if I also give her instructions on how to operate the office coffee pot.

"Hello, Palm Beach," Natalie says, answering the phone.

By 11 a.m., she's already pestering me to take her to lunch. I cave in a half-hour later.

"McDonald's," she says.

"No."

"They have salads for you," she says.

"No."

McDonald's isn't an occasion. We're going to a Greek diner, I tell her. Trust dad.

She's impressed. Especially with the red Jell-O.

You can't get red Jell-O cubes at McDonald's.

The afternoon is a complex travelogue of multiple trips to the office vending machines, the bathroom and the nearby construction site. Somewhere along the line, I realize that she's the only thing I can think about or write about today.

"I'm going to a meeting!" she says excitedly, rushing off into an editors meeting.

I start typing my column. The one about her.

She's back at my desk in 30 seconds.

Remember this, Natalie, I want to tell her.

Meetings, bad; red Jell-O, good.

And forget about Oklahoma or shaving.

"Daddy, when can we go and get a snack?"

"Right now."

Frank faces his final corral: The Men Pen
February 12, 1993

The future is now: Wives shop until husbands drop off

Living in South Florida is like being in the middle of Charles Dickens' *A Christmas Carol*.

I saw my future the other day at a shopping center in Boca Raton. And like poor Scrooge, I was served with a grim preview.

"There I am," I said to my wife. "Over there. That's me 30 years from now." We were walking by a T.J. Maxx store, where two grandfatherly looking men were sitting in the vestibule chairs.

Both were asleep, their mouths open, their heads lolling in contorted positions, their bodies angling away from each other like a human pair of TV rabbit ears.

Death by shopping.

"No," she said half-heartedly. "That won't be you."

"Oh, yes," I said. "It's just a matter of time."

She'll be inside spending our COLA money — if there is such a thing as Social Security by then — and I'll be sitting in the front of stores in those chairs they have for superfluous husbands, dreaming of . . . who knows? . . . solid food, maybe.

I call these waiting areas "men pens." And they'll be, I expect, one of my final corrals in the rodeo of senior citizenhood.

I used to shop, although it's getting to be a fuzzy memory. I would voluntarily walk in a store, touch the merchandise and occasionally buy things. Even clothes.

But over time, that ability has significantly atrophied.

I have Toxic Shop Syndrome.

I don't mind walking outside a store window, but I hate to go in. It's gotten so that the only stores I enter without a sense of dread are supermarkets and bookstores.

And the two most chilling words in the English language for me have become: factory outlet.

I'd rather cruise by a cocaine corner than cross a department store cosmetics section and risk a walk-by spraying.

I'd rather mow the lawn than walk inside one of those annoying novelty stores filled with refrigerator magnets, hard-body posters and gag gifts for people turning 40.

I'm prone to grand mall seizures — sudden urges to wait in the car rather than risk a cheerful "Can I help you?" from a clerk.

My wife, on the other hand, is like most women I know. Her shopping capability just improves with age. Some of it's out of necessity — because I'm such a load.

But there's a certain shop-till-you-drop glow that radiates from her when she's out there among the price tags.

She's a power browser who knows the meaning of the words "fully returnable." Only Pickett's men at Gettysburg have charged with more abandon.

And that's why I see men pens in my future.

I'm still young enough to resist. While she shops, I can do something with the kids, take a walk or go find something to eat.

But one day the kids will be grown, the food I want to eat will be off-limits and my energy will be rationed in short bursts.

And then I'll be ready for herding into a men pen. I'll be like Jim Leibowitz, 74, who was waiting for his wife, Lillian, while she shopped at Loehmann's in Somerset Shoppes in Boca Raton.

Loehmann's is a men pen mecca. The Boca one's got 13 seats — a fitting design touch.

Beyond the pen, schools of women shoppers were weaving in and out of the racks, feeding off a fabric coral reef.

"I don't mind," Leibowitz said from the men pen. "I'm resting. When I was younger, I would have nothing to do with this. She would have to go on her own. But I'm retired now. I've got the time.

"She's what they call a comparison buyer," he said. "She's got three closets; I've got one."

Talking to Leibowitz, who is exactly double my age, is the closest I've come to seeing a fortuneteller.

"Never say `No,' to them," he said. "It won't work. It just makes things worse.

"So I say, 'If you like it, buy it.' "

In another chair, a guy named Hyman looked at his watch: "She said it would be a half hour. It's already 45 minutes. Men can do without things. But women always need something."

Wisdom from The Ghosts of Shopping Future.

CHAPTER 17

Notes from hell
Sparring with readers

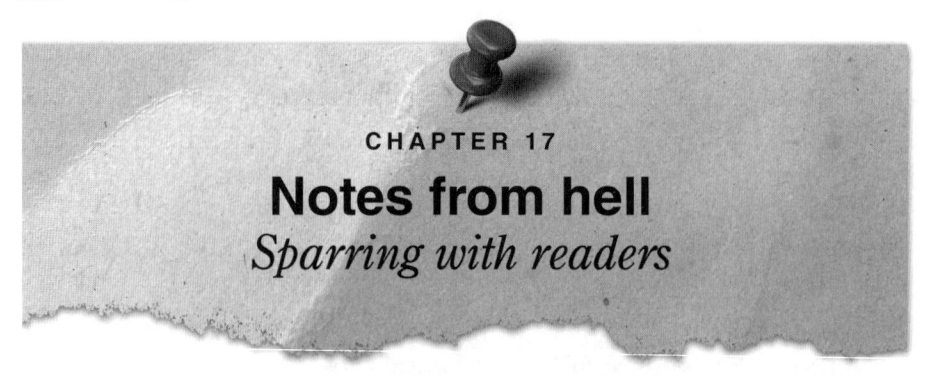

**Notes from hell, Volume 13:
An 'infestation of New Yorkers' swarms Frank's mailbox**
Nov. 28, 1993

Trashy insults, flat-tire threats, all in a day's work

I've reached a watershed in notes from helldom this month. I got my first nasty letter from a *Palm Beach Post* employee. Perhaps next month my mother will think of something snide to write.

Mark Parker, from the paper's Lake Worth distribution warehouse, got right to business, starting with the salutation.

"Dear Frank Cerabean pole."

A clear sign that he was swinging from his heels. But that was about all that was clear. Although I did appreciate the legible printing, Mark. And that line about putting me "in a vat of urine" was quite vivid.

You must keep them in stitches at the warehouse.

As for the rest of your letter, you have my condolences that — as you put it — you have to "deliver my trash every day."

Chin up, Mark. It's only three days a week.

Last month, I wrote a column about the potential invasion of the exotic 4-inch-long Madagascar hissing cockroach. In the column, I made the astute observation that once a few of them take hold in this warm, hospitable climate, we would soon be swarming with them.

"We could end up with the insect equivalent of the New Yorker infestation of South Florida," I wrote.

Astute to the max, I must say. I ought to know. I'm one of those

Notes from hell: Sparring with readers

infesting New Yorkers.

I got a few nasty letters from the column, but none of them confused me more than this one:

"We were offended . . . Although we are from the Midwest, specifically Ohio, we find this remark in poor taste and totally insulting to New Yorkers. Humor is a wonderful attribute, insensitive insults are inexcusable." — Bonnie and Gary Krauss, Singer Island.

Dear B & G: What's inexcusable is for people from the Midwest, specifically Ohio, to defend the dignity of New Yorkers. Let me put this as plainly as possible. I was in New York recently, and the nicest sentiment I encountered was on a button in Greenwich Village. It said: "Excuse me, but you're standing where I want to spit."

So thanks for all your Midwestern wholesomeness, but as a New Yorker might say: "Who axed ya'?"

New Yorkers are perfectly able to defend themselves. Like the letter I got from Myor Rosen of Palm Beach Gardens.

"If Mr. Cerabino's reference to an 'infestation' of New Yorkers was meant to be funny, I must be dense. If, however, his meaning was manifestly clear, it would appear that Cerabino's objection to the immigration of northerners — particularly New Yorkers — to these sunny shores is showing.

"Perhaps when he realizes the potential readership of all those New Yorkers who bring with them their heightened love of the arts, theatre, literature, culture and social awareness, the challenge to raise his sights occasionally above that of a 4-inch Madagascar cockroach might seem daunting. Perhaps an apology would be in order." — Myor Rosen, former harpist, N.Y. Philharmonic.

Dear Myor: Professional harpist, you say. Somehow, I'm not surprised.

And speaking of tiresome people, I got a lovely letter from the Tire King himself, Chuck Curcio.

The Tire Kingdom president wrote in response to my comment that I'd love a jamming device on my television set that would prevent me from seeing any more of him and his corny tire commercials.

He responded:

"Speaking about jamming, there must be a way to jam you and

your newspaper. By jove, I've got it, perhaps thousands of roofing nails dumped each day at The Post *delivery terminals. Of course, Tire Kingdom will be happy to repair these flats free of charge, except for yours, Frank. All you get is a song and a dance. Then you'll really be jammin'."* — Chuck Curcio.

Dear Chuck: First of all, as for the suggestion that you'd do anything free of charge, be advised that I'm forwarding that information to the attorney general's song-and-dance division.

And finally, Chuck, let me warn you about something else in your letter. If you decide to spread those roofing nails near the Lake Worth delivery terminal, beware of my good friend, Mark Parker. My guess is, he's getting near the end of his wick. If he mentions the vat of urine, you'd better run.

Notes from hell, Volume 19:
Frank's face on lunch box equals fresh form of hell
March 5, 1995

'Old man' gives students advice but dodges spots A through G

"I read in today's paper that a woman was shot and the bullet is in her yet . . . Where is a woman's `yet'?" — Donald Shannon, Lake Worth.

Dear Donald: Beats me. Women apparently have all sorts of nooks and crannies I don't know about.

I learned a few years ago that they have something called a "G spot." (To add to my dismay, I had no clue as to the whereabouts of spots A through F.)

As for the "yet," all I can say is that I'm pretty sure I haven't found it. I know this because my wife keeps telling me, "Not yet. Not yet."

"A classmate of mine, Ed Skrod, is such a fan of yours that your picture from the paper is taped prominently on his Igloo cooler lunch box." — Margie Beuttenmuller, Cardinal Newman High School.

Dear Margie: Thanks for the warning. I've heard some troubling tales from the halls of local high schools — gangs, guns, pregnancies, lunch — but nothing as chilling as this.

If you run into Ed, and believe me, I'm not suggesting you do, please tell him that it might not be too late for him to get a life. Be careful — Frank.

"Thanks for taking the time to write a letter to my friend Margie Beuttenmuller . . . Frank, I'm hurt. You destroyed my hopes, dreams and expectations of becoming a satirical old man like you . . . Here is a picture of me for your lunch box." — Ed Skrod, Jupiter.

Dear Ed: I may have underestimated you. That "old man like you" line was a paper cut on my soul. I'm a pretty good judge of character, Ed, and after reading your letter, I can tell that you're someone who's going places.

Hopefully, out of state.

Perhaps while on your journey you'll find out where the "yet" is. If you do, let me know.

But I'll give you a suggestion, Ed. You're never going to find out where "yet" is if you walk around with my face displayed on the side of your lunch box.

As for that handsome photo of you posing in front of your fireplace: I'm going to have to decline your suggestion that I put it on my lunch box — assuming, Ed, I even have a lunch box. (Do you think I work in an automobile plant?)

Don't take it personally, Ed. But in the current social climate, when an "old man" like me puts the photo of a young Turk like you on his lunch box, somebody's going to drop a dime to an anonymous hotline number. Playing it safe — Frank.

"Having practically given up on Frank Cerabino ever writing anything worth reading, I was delighted to read his recent article concerning the tobacco issue . . . One can only hope that this is just the beginning of a new Cerabino who uses logic rather than caustic humor to make a point." — Louis Adiano, Lake Worth.

Dear Louis: I'm hurt to practically Skrodian proportions over your suggestion that my columns are chronically void of logic. To remedy that, I'll try to answer your letter in mathematical form.

Let A equal the value of Louis Adiano's opinion

Let B equal the percentage chance that there is "a new Cerabino."

Let C equal the total number of Ed Skrod photos on my lunch box.

Let pi equal blueberry.

Using the above information, Louis, I will now answer your letter in an equation.

Answer: $A + B = C$

Making a point — Frank.

"I don't know what the world is coming to when I find myself agreeing with you." — Carole Parsons, Palm Beach Gardens.

Dear Carole: To borrow a phrase from my logical chum, Louis Adiano, perhaps we're witnessing "the beginning of a new Parsons."

"I've always wondered if you have ever written a 'Notes from heaven' column." — Rebecca Adams, West Palm Beach.

Dear Rebecca: Your letter is written with the assumption that I get a lot of glowing mail, an assumption that Mr. Adiano would find illogical.

But what concerns me, Rebecca, is that you'd want to read happy mail. A disturbing thought.

I noticed from your letter that, like my pal, Ed Skrod, you are also a local high school student.

Forgive me, but I think I can help you both.

You need an edge. Ed's got an edge.

Ed needs a life. He doesn't need me on his lunch box. He needs someone like you.

So here's the plan, Rebecca. You send me your photo. I send it to Ed. He rips me off his Igloo, and puts you on. I send you the fireplace photo of Ed.

Ed gets a life. You get Skrodian *Weltschmerz*.

And I get a little peace. Well, maybe not.

Not yet.

Notes from hell, Volume 33:
He's pitiful! Pugnacious! And non-photogenic!
Aug. 2, 1998

'The Right Man' is better-looking right about noon

"The Palm Beach Post employs a writer whose byline is Frank Cerabino. His commentary consists largely of writing derogatory observations about Florida places and people. If his function at The Post *is to irritate readers, to that extent, you have the right man."* — Warren Blackmon, Fort Pierce.

Dear Mr. Blackmon: Thank you for your letter, Warren. It couldn't have come at a better time. I'm planning to ask my editor for a raise, and I'd like to use your letter as evidence of what a good job I'm doing.

I'm condensing your comments, just a tad, in order to convey your heartfelt sentiments more succinctly. Don't worry. I won't take your words out of context.

Here's what I've come up with: "Frank Cerabino . . . the right man."

I hope this accurately captures the essence of your remarks.

"I pray God will continue to provide you with much material to write your column for many years to come." — Doris Lindstrom, Palm Springs.

Dear Mrs. Lindstrom: Don't worry, Doris. God apparently has an unlimited supply of derogatory observations about Florida places and people.

"I previously discontinued delivery of your paper because of the lack of newsworthy stories and the ridiculous amount of space you gave to Cerabino, probably the most pitiful columnist in the business." — Diana Fay, Boynton Beach

Dear Mrs. Fay: I hope you're insured against plagues of locusts.

"You are much better looking than the picture in the paper! (the one in the column)." — Agatha Berger, Boynton Beach

Dear Agatha: My good friend, Diana Fay in Boynton Beach, thinks the words in my column are awful. And now you, Agatha, thinks the column photo stinks, too.

But other than the words and photo, you ladies have no complaints. That's good.

"If you hear of a nice furnished room that a senior as myself could afford near the beach, I would certainly appreciate the information. And as a finder's reward I promise you a free-bee visit to the Mermaid Lounge in West Palm Beach." — Max Wolff, Englewood, N.J.

Dear Mr. Wolff: I may be one of the most pitiful columnists in the business, but I haven't gotten to the point where I'd use my column to find snowbirds cheap winter rentals near the beach.

If you think I'd stoop to notifying landlords that you only need the rental for January and February, and that they can reach me during working hours at extension 4421, you've got another thing coming!

And Mr. Wolff, as for your offer to compensate me by treating me to a visit to one of our local strip clubs, let me just say that it would be highly unethical of me to accept an offer like this. And it would be something I'd be well-advised to turn down, especially since you didn't indicate whether an all-expenses-paid lap dance would be included in the package. Just wondering.

"On what premise is the state law based that no beer or wine can be sold in supermarkets before 12 noon on Sundays? . . . Is this law meant to keep winos in church?" — Kathleen Montgomery

Dear Kathleen: Only God knows, and he's kind of busy right now, trying to help me out with this pitiful column by supplying me with derogatory observations about Floridians, while I'm otherwise occupied, screening landlord calls for Mr. Wolff and trying to convince my editor that I'm "the right man" for the job, and that readers would like me better if only my column photo looked more lifelike and less like a guy who just misplaced his Viagra prescription.

Jeez! It's enough to make a guy want to start drinking before noon.

BEING FRANK

Frank Cerabino grew up on Long Island, New York, and graduated from the United States Naval Academy at Annapolis, Md., in 1977. After spending five years as a Naval officer, Cerabino earned a master's degree in journalism from Northwestern University, in Evanston, Ill., and worked as a reporter at a Chicago wire service.

Cerabino moved to South Florida in 1984 to write for *The Miami Herald*. Five years later, Cerabino joined *The Palm Beach Post* as a general assignment reporter. He began writing columns for the newspaper during the William Kennedy Smith trial in 1991, and has since written three-to-five columns a week for the Local News section of *The Post*. The newspaper has also serialized Cerabino's comic novels, *Shady Palms* and *Pelican Park*.

He is a married father of three children and lives in Boca Raton.